Stoicism at the Summit

Embodying Ancient Principles for Peak Performance and Leadership in Business

Greig Calder

Kirsten Calder

Disclaimer

This book is intended for informational and educational purposes only. The authors make no representations or warranties of any kind, express or implied, about the completeness, accuracy, reliability, suitability or availability with respect to the book or the information or related graphics contained in the book for any purpose. Any reliance you place on such information is therefore strictly at your own risk.

The authors do not assume any responsibility for errors, inaccuracies or omissions. They shall not be liable for any loss or damage of any kind, including but not limited to any direct, indirect, incidental, consequential, special or exemplary damages, arising from or in connection with the use of the book or the information contained within it.

All characters and organisations in the case studies are fictional. Any resemblance to real persons, living or dead, is purely coincidental.

ISBN: 9798866774128

Contents

Step 3
Climbing with Stoic Leadership

Chapter 5:
Lead Like a Stoic: Unshakeable and Wise.....................49

Chapter 6:
Building and Leading Stoic Teams: Strategies for
Sustainable Success..64

Step 4
Strategies and Execution

Chapter 7:
Stoic Strategies for Sustainable Business Growth.........87

Chapter 8:
Making Informed and Ethical Decisions: A Stoic Approach...107

Step 5
Realising Stoic Principles in Business Operations

Chapter 9:
Transforming Theory into Practice: Stoicism in Daily Operations...135

Introduction
The Stoic Ladder to Business Excellence

In the relentless pursuit of excellence, businesses often navigate treacherous terrains, facing unpredictable challenges and ever-shifting goals. The corporate world can seem like a mountain, one that requires not just skill and strategy but also a certain mindset to climb. How does one stay grounded in the face of adversity, maintain equanimity amidst the chaos, and lead with unwavering purpose and integrity? The answer might lie not in modern management books but in an ancient philosophy: Stoicism.

Stoicism, a Hellenistic philosophy that thrived in ancient Greece and Rome, has been a guiding light for thinkers, leaders, and achievers for centuries. Rooted in rationality, self-control, and virtue, Stoicism is more than just an academic idea; it's a way of life that offers tangible strategies for real-world challenges. In the arena of business, where stakes are high and margins for error slim, Stoicism provides a ladder – a step-by-step guide to ascending the summit of business excellence.

The **Stoic Ladder to Business Excellence** is not just a metaphor but a structured path:

1. **Grasping Stoicism** is our foundational step. Before implementing its principles in the business realm, it's vital to understand Stoicism's core tenets, ethics, and virtues. Like any journey, knowing our tools and maps ensures we're well-prepared for the climb.

2. Developing a **Stoic Mindset** is the next phase. It's not enough to merely know Stoic principles; one must internalise them. This step focuses on cultivating a mental

landscape that is resilient, balanced, and anchored in Stoic virtues, setting the stage for effective leadership and decision-making.

3. **Climbing with Stoic Leadership** explores how to translate the Stoic mindset into actionable leadership strategies. How does a Stoic leader behave? How can teams benefit from Stoic principles? This step delves into leadership that is not just effective but also ethical and sustainable.

4. The phase on **Strategies and Execution** discusses the tangible aspects of running a business through a Stoic lens. It's where theory meets practice, where decisions are made, and where the future of the business is charted. From growth strategies to ethical dilemmas, this step ensures that Stoicism isn't just a mindset but a practical tool.

5. Finally, **Realising Stoic Principles in Business Operations** is about integration. How does one ensure that every aspect of business, from daily operations to long-term planning, is imbued with Stoic principles? This step is about ensuring consistency, sustainability, and a future that's not just profitable but also principled.

As you embark on this journey through the pages of this book, envision yourself ascending a mountain. Each chapter, each section, is a rung on the Stoic ladder, leading you closer to the summit of business excellence. Whether you're a budding entrepreneur, a seasoned CEO, or someone simply interested in personal development, this ladder is designed to elevate your perspective, enrich your strategies, and empower you to achieve peak performance in business and beyond. Prepare to climb. The Stoic ladder awaits.

Step 1
Grasping Stoicism

Chapter 1
Stoicism Unveiled: More Than an Ancient Philosophy

In the heart of ancient Athens, Stoicism emerged not just as a philosophy but as a way of life. It promised solace to the troubled, direction to the lost, and wisdom to the seeker. But what is Stoicism, and why does a philosophy that predates the modern business world by millennia remain relevant today? Let's unveil the layers of Stoicism, revealing its essence and the profound impact it can have on our contemporary lives, especially in the realm of business.

Origins of Stoicism

The origins of Stoicism can be traced back to a bustling Athens, a city-state that was not just the cradle of democracy but also a melting pot of ideas, debates, and intellectual pursuits. To truly understand Stoicism's genesis, it's essential to journey back to this vibrant period in history and meet the personalities that shaped its core tenets.

Zeno of Citium: The Founder
Zeno, born around 334 BCE in Citium (modern-day Cyprus), was initially a merchant. Legend has it that Zeno ended up in Athens after a shipwreck, where he chanced upon a bookstore and was introduced to the teachings of Socrates. This serendipitous event changed the course of his life. He became an avid student of philosophy, studying under the Cynic Crates and later, other philosophical traditions like Megarian and Academic.

It was in the painted stoa (a colonnade or porch) of Athens that Zeno began teaching his synthesis of these philosophies, giving birth to the term "Stoicism," derived from the Greek word "stoa."

Philosophical Influences

1. Socratic Teachings: Socrates, though never having written down his teachings, significantly impacted Stoicism through his emphasis on virtue and ethics. His belief that no one commits wrong willingly and that knowledge can lead to virtue resonated deeply with Stoic principles.

2. Cynicism: The Cynics, with their disdain for materialism and societal conventions, emphasised living in accordance with nature. This idea was foundational to Stoicism, albeit with a more structured and less radical approach.

3. Megarian School: From the Megarians, Stoicism inherited dialectical reasoning and logic, which became one of its three central pillars.

The Stoa Poikile: A School for All

Zeno's teachings in the Stoa Poikile (Painted Porch) of Athens were open to all. Unlike some other schools of thought, Stoicism was remarkably inclusive, welcoming students regardless of their social status, wealth, or origin. This inclusivity mirrored the Stoic belief in the brotherhood of humanity and the universal rationality that binds all.

Legacy and Successors

While Zeno laid Stoicism's foundations, it was his successors who expanded and refined it. Cleanthes, Zeno's immediate successor as the head of the Stoic school, is best known for his Hymn to Zeus, which encapsulates Stoic theology and the idea of living in accordance with divine reason. Following Cleanthes, Chrysippus took over the school's reins, and his extensive writings (though largely lost to time) solidified much of Stoic doctrine. He is often credited with systematising Stoic teachings and making significant contributions to Stoic logic and ethics.

The origins of Stoicism, rooted in the dynamic intellectual environment of ancient Athens, reflect a synthesis of various philosophical traditions. Its emergence was not just the result of Zeno's teachings but a confluence of ideas that resonated deeply with the challenges and aspirations of the time. As we understand Stoicism's origins, it becomes evident that it was never a static or dogmatic philosophy. Instead, it evolved, adapted, and grew, always staying relevant to the needs of the society it served. This adaptability is perhaps why Stoicism remains pertinent even today, offering timeless wisdom in an ever-changing world.

The Pillars of Stoicism

The robustness of Stoicism as a philosophy is anchored in its three fundamental pillars: Logic, Physics, and Ethics. These pillars serve as the foundation upon which the entire Stoic worldview is built. Each pillar complements the others, creating a holistic approach to understanding the universe, our place in it, and how we ought to live. Let's delve deeper into each of these pillars to understand their significance and interconnectedness.

1. Logic: The Structure of Reason

Stoicism places a high premium on rational thought and the pursuit of knowledge. Logic, in the Stoic context, is not just about formal reasoning but encompasses the processes of thinking, judging, and discerning.

Dialectic: Stoics believed in the art of dialectic, a form of structured dialogue or argument to uncover truth. This method was used to refine beliefs, challenge assumptions, and arrive at a clearer understanding of the world and human nature.

Propositional Logic: The Stoics developed an early form of propositional logic, examining how statements and propositions can be combined to form arguments. Their contributions in this area laid the groundwork for later advancements in logic and philosophy.

Epistemology: Stoicism also delved into the nature and limits of human knowledge. Stoics held that certain knowledge was possible through 'clear impressions,' which are perceptions so evident and distinct that they cannot be doubted.

2. Physics: Understanding the Cosmos

While the term 'physics' might conjure images of modern scientific study, Stoic physics is a blend of natural science, theology, and metaphysics. It's about understanding the nature of the universe and the forces that govern it.

Cosmology: Stoics believed that the universe is a rational, ordered entity. Everything is interconnected, and events unfold according to a divine plan or 'Logos.' This deterministic view held that everything happens for a reason, even if we, with our limited perspective, cannot always discern it.

Materialism: In Stoic physics, the universe is purely material. Even the soul, though divine, is composed of a finer kind of matter. This perspective ties back to their belief in a unified, tangible cosmos where everything has substance.

Pantheism: Stoics viewed the universe itself as a living entity, with the divine permeating everything. God, or the Logos, was not separate from the world but was the very reason and order inherent in it.

3. Ethics: The Art of Living Well

Arguably the most influential pillar for individuals, Stoic ethics is about understanding how to live a good life. It's a guide for behaviour, decision-making, and cultivating one's character.

Virtue as the Highest Good: Stoics believed that virtue is the only true good and that external circumstances, whether considered traditionally 'good' or 'bad', are indifferent in terms of leading a good life.

Cardinal Virtues: Central to Stoic ethics are the four cardinal virtues: wisdom (correct knowledge and judgment), courage (facing challenges with integrity), justice (fairness and right action), and temperance (self-control and moderation). These virtues serve as guidelines for every aspect of life.

Eudaimonia: The ultimate goal of Stoic ethics is eudaimonia, often translated as 'flourishing' or 'living in accordance with nature.' For Stoics, this means living rationally, in harmony with the universe, and embodying the cardinal virtues.

The three pillars of Stoicism, while distinct, are intricately intertwined. Logic informs our understanding of the world (Physics) and how we should act within it (Ethics). Similarly, our understanding of the universe (Physics) shapes our reasoning (Logic) and dictates our moral choices (Ethics). This holistic approach ensures that Stoicism is not just a theoretical philosophy but a practical guide for living a meaningful, purposeful life.

Stoicism and Modern Misconceptions

In today's lexicon, the word "stoic" often conjures images of an emotionless individual, seemingly indifferent to joy, sorrow, and everything in between. Yet, this contemporary interpretation is a far cry from the rich tapestry of Stoic philosophy and its nuanced approach to emotions and life. Delving deeper into this, we uncover the modern misconceptions surrounding Stoicism and bring to light its true essence.

Misconception 1: Stoics are Emotionless

One of the most prevalent misconceptions is that Stoicism advocates for the suppression or elimination of emotions. This idea stems from the modern use of the word "stoic" to describe someone who is unemotional or impassive.

Reality: Stoics do not deny emotions. Instead, they advocate for understanding, managing, and channeling them in constructive ways. Stoicism teaches emotional mastery, allowing individuals to experience feelings without being overwhelmed or controlled by them.

Misconception 2: Stoicism Means Accepting All Outcomes Passively

Many believe that Stoics accept all events, even injustices, without resistance, equating Stoicism with passivity.

Reality: Stoics do emphasise accepting things outside of one's control, but this doesn't mean passive resignation. Stoics believe in taking proactive, virtuous actions in areas they can influence while maintaining inner peace regarding outcomes beyond their control.

Misconception 3: Stoicism is Pessimistic

Given the Stoic practices like "premeditatio malorum" (premeditation of evils), where one contemplates potential negative events, some label Stoicism as a gloomy or pessimistic philosophy.

Reality: Such practices are not about cultivating negativity but fostering resilience. By considering potential challenges, Stoics prepare themselves mentally, ensuring they're not caught off guard. This forward-thinking approach is more about realistic preparation than pessimism.

Misconception 4: Stoicism is Just for Men

Historical references often highlight male Stoic philosophers and practitioners, leading to a modern misconception that Stoicism is a male-centric philosophy.

Reality: While many historical texts feature male Stoics due to the gender biases of ancient times, Stoic principles are universal. Stoicism speaks to human experiences and challenges, making its teachings relevant and accessible to all, regardless of gender.

Misconception 5: Stoicism Promotes Isolation

Given the Stoic emphasis on self-sufficiency and inner peace, some believe that Stoicism encourages individuals to distance themselves from society and relationships.
Reality: Stoics value community and relationships deeply. They believe in the idea of "cosmopolitanism" – viewing all humans as part of a single, interconnected community. While Stoics emphasise inner contentment, they also recognise the importance of social bonds and communal responsibilities.

Like many ancient philosophies, Stoicism is often misunderstood in the modern era, with its teachings sometimes oversimplified or misinterpreted. However, by debunking these misconceptions, we can appreciate Stoicism's depth and relevance. It's not a doctrine of emotional suppression or passive acceptance but a rich guide for leading a balanced, virtuous, and meaningful life. As we continue to explore Stoicism in subsequent chapters, we'll further unravel its layers, appreciating its timeless wisdom in both personal and professional realms.

Stoicism in Today's Business Landscape

In a rapidly changing global economy, where businesses face unprecedented challenges and opportunities, ancient Stoicism might seem out of place. Yet, this millennia-old philosophy has found renewed relevance among CEOs, entrepreneurs, and professionals. Let's explore why Stoicism resonates so profoundly in today's corporate world and how its principles can guide businesses towards sustainable success.

Navigating Uncertainty with Equanimity

Today's businesses operate in volatile environments, with fluctuating markets, technological disruptions, and geopolitical shifts.

Stoic Principle: Stoics believe in focusing on what's within one's control and accepting what isn't. By distinguishing between these, leaders can maintain composure, making decisions with clarity rather than reacting impulsively to external pressures.

Ethical Decision-Making in Business

With global scrutiny and a demand for corporate responsibility, businesses can no longer afford to prioritise profits over ethics.

Stoic Principle: Stoic ethics, centred on virtues like wisdom, justice, and integrity, provides a moral compass. A Stoic leader would weigh decisions against these virtues, ensuring actions align with ethical standards and long-term sustainability.

Resilience in the Face of Challenges

Every business faces setbacks, be it financial downturns, competitive pressures, or internal conflicts.

Stoic Principle: Stoicism teaches resilience through emotional mastery. Instead of being swayed by immediate emotions, Stoic leaders view challenges as opportunities for growth, learning from failures and adapting with agility.

Long-Term Vision Over Short-Term Gains

The pressure for quarterly results can sometimes lead businesses to prioritise short-term gains over long-term sustainability.

Stoic Principle: Stoics advocate for a broader perspective, focusing on long-term goals and the bigger picture. This approach ensures businesses remain sustainable, building lasting value rather than fleeting successes.

Building Cohesive and Harmonious Teams
In diverse corporate environments, managing interpersonal dynamics and ensuring team cohesion is crucial.
Stoic Principle: Stoicism's idea of cosmopolitanism – seeing all humans as part of a universal brotherhood – promotes understanding and collaboration. Stoic leaders foster inclusive environments, valuing each team member's contributions and ensuring harmonious collaborations.

Continuous Personal and Professional Growth
In a competitive landscape, continuous growth and adaptation are vital for businesses and professionals.
Stoic Principle: Stoicism emphasises self-reflection and personal development. Leaders who embrace Stoic teachings are committed to continuous learning, seeking feedback, and striving for both personal and organisational betterment.

Stoicism, with its emphasis on rationality, ethics, and inner fortitude, offers invaluable insights for the modern business world. It's not just about individual tranquility but about building businesses that are resilient, ethical, and successful. As we further delve into Stoicism's tenets in subsequent chapters, we'll discover actionable strategies and insights that can transform business challenges into opportunities and lead organisations towards a path of sustainable excellence.

Conclusion

As we journeyed through the annals of time, uncovering Stoicism's origins and dissecting its core tenets, one thing becomes abundantly clear: Stoicism is not a relic of the past, but a vibrant, living philosophy with profound implications for the present and future. Its principles, rooted in rationality, ethics, and the pursuit of inner harmony, resonate deeply with the challenges and aspirations of contemporary life, especially in the business realm.

In a world inundated with information yet starved for wisdom, Stoicism stands as a beacon of clarity. It offers not just theoretical knowledge, but practical tools for navigating the complexities of modern existence. From managing personal emotions to steering colossal corporations, the Stoic approach provides a balanced, grounded perspective, emphasising virtues that are often sidelined in the frenetic rush of contemporary life.

For business professionals, Stoicism presents a unique proposition: a fusion of ethical integrity with strategic prowess. It's a call to lead with both the head and the heart, to make decisions rooted in long-term vision and moral responsibility, and to view challenges not as insurmountable obstacles, but as opportunities for growth and learning.

But this chapter is merely the beginning, a doorway into the vast and enriching realm of Stoic thought. As we continue our exploration in subsequent chapters, we'll delve deeper into how Stoicism can be practically applied, transforming abstract concepts into actionable strategies. Whether you're a seasoned entrepreneur, an emerging leader, or someone seeking personal enlightenment, the Stoic path promises insights, growth, and a renewed sense of purpose.

In embracing Stoicism, we don't just uncover an ancient philosophy; we discover a timeless guide for living and leading with wisdom, virtue, and purpose. As we step forward, let us carry with us the Stoic tenets, allowing them to illuminate our path, enrich our decisions, and empower our journey towards excellence in both business and life.

Chapter 2
Navigating Through Stoic Ethics and Virtues

As we tread deeper into the realm of Stoicism, one cannot help but be drawn to its ethical core. Stoicism is not merely a philosophy of thought, but one of action. It beckons us to live in alignment with specific virtues, guiding our daily choices and interactions. This chapter unravels the rich tapestry of Stoic ethics and virtues, offering a roadmap for a life led with purpose, integrity, and wisdom.

The Heart of Stoic Ethics

Stoic ethics, often encapsulated in the phrase "living in accordance with nature," is a compass that directs one's life towards harmony, purpose, and virtue. But this notion of "nature" transcends the physical environment around us; it delves into the very essence of existence, human nature, and the rational order of the universe.

For the Stoics, the universe operates with a profound rationality and purpose, often referred to as the "Logos." This divine reason or cosmic logic underscores every event, every interaction, and every moment. Thus, to live in accordance with nature is to align one's actions, decisions, and mindset with this universal reason, to recognise our place in the grand tapestry of existence and to act with purpose, understanding, and virtue.

Humans, endowed with reason, have the unique capacity to recognise this cosmic order and consciously align with it. This alignment isn't just about external actions but an internal state of being, where one's values, intentions, and actions are in harmony with the world's rational structure.

The famous Stoic philosopher, Seneca, once said, *"If a man knows not which port he sails, no wind is favourable."* This quote encapsulates the Stoic emphasis on purposeful living. Without understanding the larger order and our role within it, our actions lack direction. By aligning with the Stoic understanding of nature, we find our "port" or purpose and can navigate life's challenges with clarity and conviction.

Another illuminating quote comes from Marcus Aurelius, a Roman emperor and Stoic philosopher, who wrote in his 'Meditations': *"Everything harmonises with me, which is harmonious to thee, O Universe. Nothing for me is too early or too late, which is in due time for thee."* This reflects the Stoic belief in accepting the unfolding of events as part of a greater cosmic plan, emphasising the serenity that comes from understanding and aligning with the universe's natural rhythms.

The heart of Stoic ethics, rooted in living in harmony with the universe's rational order, offers a profound perspective on life. It calls us to transcend fleeting desires and impulses, urging us to seek deeper understanding, purpose, and alignment with the cosmic order. In this alignment, we find not just clarity and direction but also a profound peace, knowing that our actions resonate with the universe's timeless rhythm.

The Four Cardinal Virtues

The Stoic philosophy, while vast and encompassing, is anchored in four cardinal virtues. These virtues serve as the guiding stars, illuminating the path to a life of purpose, integrity, and wisdom. They are not mere theoretical constructs but practical tools for daily living, providing clarity in moments of doubt and strength in times of adversity. Let's delve deeper into each virtue, understanding its essence and its relevance in our lives.

Wisdom (Sophia)
Wisdom transcends mere knowledge. It represents the ability to discern what is right, to judge correctly, and to act accordingly. Wisdom is the virtue of the philosopher, the seeker, and the lifelong learner. It's about recognising the deeper truths of existence and navigating life's complexities with clarity and insight.

Epictetus once remarked, *"It's not what happens to you, but how you react to it that matters."* This encapsulates the Stoic emphasis on wisdom – the ability to perceive events with clarity, understand their nature, and respond with reasoned judgment.

Courage (Andreia)
Courage in Stoicism is multifaceted. It's not just the bravery of a soldier in battle but the moral courage to stand for what's right, even when it's challenging. Courage is about facing life's adversities head-on, whether they are external challenges or internal struggles, with unwavering resolve.

Seneca, in his letters, wrote: *"Sometimes even to live is an act of courage."* This profound statement underscores the Stoic belief that true courage is found not just in grand gestures but in the daily act of living, especially when faced with hardships.

Justice (Dikaiosyne):
Justice, for the Stoics, is more than just legal righteousness. It's about harmony in relationships, fairness in dealings, and ensuring the well-being of both the individual and the community. Justice calls for treating each individual with dignity and respect, recognising the inherent worth of every human being.

Reflecting on justice and our interconnectedness, Marcus Aurelius noted, *"What is harmful to the hive is harmful to the bee."* This emphasises the Stoic belief in the interdependence of individuals and the larger community, highlighting the importance of just actions for the collective good.

Temperance (Sophrosyne):
Often misunderstood, temperance is not about mere restraint or self-denial. It's the virtue of balance, moderation, and self-control. Temperance ensures that our desires, emotions, and actions are in harmony, preventing excesses and ensuring a balanced approach to life.

Epictetus provides insight into this virtue by saying, *"Freedom is not achieved by satisfying desire, but by eliminating it."* This speaks to the heart of temperance – the idea that true freedom and contentment come from mastering our desires, not being enslaved by them.

The four cardinal virtues of Stoicism serve as a moral compass, guiding individuals towards a life of purpose, virtue, and harmony. They are not just ideals to aspire to but practical principles for daily living. By embodying these virtues, one aligns with the Stoic ideal of living in accordance with nature, achieving a state of eudaimonia, or flourishing. As we continue our exploration of Stoicism, these virtues will emerge as the bedrock upon which the entire philosophy stands, offering timeless insights for personal growth, ethical living, and profound contentment.

Navigating Life with Stoic Virtues

The Stoic virtues, while profound in their implications, are not just theoretical ideals. They are practical tools, guiding lights that illuminate our path as we navigate the intricate maze of life. Whether we're facing personal dilemmas, professional challenges, or existential questions, these virtues offer clarity, strength, and direction. Let's delve deeper into how these virtues can shape our daily experiences, decisions, and interactions.

Decision Making with Wisdom

In the face of countless choices, wisdom acts as our internal compass. It encourages us to seek knowledge, reflect on our experiences, and discern the best course of action. Whether it's a personal life choice or a business strategy, wisdom calls for a blend of knowledge, experience, and intuition. It reminds us to weigh the implications, foresee potential consequences, and choose paths that align with our core values.

Facing Challenges with Courage

Life is replete with challenges – unexpected setbacks, personal struggles, and external adversities. Courage, in this context, is not just about confronting these challenges head-on but doing so with resilience, conviction, and a positive mindset. It's the courage to persist in the face of failure, to voice unpopular opinions, or to venture into the unknown. In business, this could mean launching a novel product, entering an uncharted market, or upholding ethical standards amidst pressures.

Building Relationships with Justice

Our lives are defined by our relationships – with family, friends, colleagues, and the broader community. Justice ensures that these relationships are rooted in fairness, respect, and understanding. It's about recognising the inherent value of every individual, treating them with dignity, and fostering mutual trust. In professional settings, justice manifests as equitable treatment of employees, transparent dealings with stakeholders, and a commitment to corporate social responsibility.

Maintaining Balance with Temperance

In a world that often celebrates excess – be it wealth, fame, or indulgence – temperance is a gentle reminder of the beauty of balance. It's about enjoying life's pleasures without becoming enslaved by them, managing our desires, and seeking a middle path. Temperance ensures that we don't get swayed by transient emotions or fleeting temptations. It promotes a balanced lifestyle, avoiding the pitfalls of overindulgence or extreme austerity.

Personal Growth and Reflection
The Stoic virtues also guide our personal development journey. They encourage self-reflection, introspection, and continuous learning. Wisdom pushes us to seek knowledge and broaden our horizons. Courage motivates us to step out of our comfort zones, embracing new experiences and challenges. Justice reminds us of our responsibilities towards the community, urging us to give back and make a positive impact. Temperance ensures that our personal growth is balanced, holistic, and sustainable.

Navigating life with Stoic virtues is like having a map for a complex terrain. These virtues don't promise a life devoid of challenges, but they offer the tools to face them with grace, resilience, and purpose. By internalising and practicing these virtues, we can lead lives of profound meaning, making decisions that resonate with our core values, building relationships rooted in trust and respect, and continuously evolving as individuals. The Stoic path, illuminated by these virtues, beckons us to a life of depth, purpose, and profound contentment.

Conclusion

As we've journeyed through the landscape of Stoic ethics and virtues, we've unearthed more than just ancient philosophical tenets; we've discovered timeless principles that resonate deeply with the human experience. These virtues, though articulated centuries ago, hold an enduring relevance, acting as beacons guiding us through the complexities of modern life.

The essence of Stoicism is not about detachment from the world but a deeper engagement with it. It's about embracing life in all its hues, navigating its challenges with equanimity, and celebrating its joys with moderation. The Stoic virtues of wisdom, courage, justice, and temperance are not mere philosophical constructs but actionable guidelines that can shape our daily decisions, interactions, and aspirations.

In a world that often feels chaotic and overwhelming, these virtues offer a sanctuary of clarity and purpose. They encourage us to reflect on our actions, to question our motivations, and to align our lives with values that transcend fleeting desires or societal pressures. Whether we're grappling with personal dilemmas, professional challenges, or societal issues, the Stoic virtues provide a framework for ethical, balanced, and meaningful responses.

Furthermore, as we've explored these virtues in the context of both personal and professional realms, it becomes evident that Stoicism is not just a personal philosophy but a holistic approach to life. Businesses, leaders, and organisations can draw immense insights from Stoicism, crafting strategies rooted in ethical integrity, long-term vision, and communal responsibility.

In embracing and embodying these virtues, we embark on a transformative journey. A journey that not only enriches our personal lives but ripples outwards, influencing our relationships, our communities, and the broader world. It's a journey towards a life of depth, purpose, and profound contentment.

As we progress through the subsequent chapters, we'll delve deeper into the practical applications of Stoicism, exploring how its teachings can be woven into the fabric of our daily lives, businesses, and societies. But as we move forward, let the four cardinal virtues be our compass, guiding us towards decisions and actions that resonate with truth, purpose, and the greater good.

Step 2
The Stoic Mindset

Chapter 3
Developing a Stoic Mindset: The First Step Towards Excellence

The power of the mind is both vast and profound, influencing every facet of our lives. From the choices we make, the challenges we overcome, to the success we achieve, it all fundamentally stems from our mindset. In both personal and professional realms, our mindset acts as the lens through which we view and interact with the world. It shapes our perceptions, guides our reactions, and sets the trajectory for our actions. A constructive mindset can elevate us to great heights, while a negative one can hinder our progress and cloud our judgment.

Enter the Stoic mindset.

Stoicism, an ancient philosophy rooted in rationality and virtue, offers a mindset that is both pragmatic and transformative. It isn't merely a set of beliefs but a way of life, a mental framework that equips us to navigate the complexities of life with equanimity, purpose, and wisdom. The Stoic mindset emphasises understanding the dichotomy of control, accepting the natural order of the universe, and focusing on personal virtue and growth.

But what truly constitutes a "Stoic mindset"? At its core, it is the cultivation of inner fortitude, the pursuit of wisdom, and the commitment to act in accordance with nature and reason. It's about recognising that while external events may be beyond our control, our reactions, judgments, and decisions lie squarely within our domain. This mindset fosters resilience, clarity, and a deep sense of purpose.

The transformative potential of adopting a Stoic mindset is immense. Personally, it paves the way for inner peace, heightened self-awareness, and meaningful relationships. Professionally, it offers leaders and teams a compass to make balanced decisions, manage challenges, and foster a culture of mutual respect and growth.

As we embark on this exploration into the Stoic mindset, we invite readers to approach it with an open heart and mind, ready to delve deep into its principles and discover its profound impact on both personal and professional excellence.

The Essence of the Stoic Mindset

The Stoic mindset, rich in depth and nuance, is anchored in a few foundational principles that have stood the test of time. These principles provide a roadmap to navigate the complexities of life, offering insights that are as relevant today as they were in ancient times.

Rationality as Our Guiding Light
At the heart of Stoicism lies a profound respect for reason and rationality. The Stoics believed that humans, by nature, are rational beings and that this rationality differentiates us from other creatures. It is this ability to reason that allows us to discern, judge, and act in harmony with nature.

"Man is not disturbed by events, but by the views he takes of them." - Epictetus

Personal Context: By harnessing our innate rationality, we can confront personal challenges, make sound decisions, and cultivate inner peace.

Business Context: In the corporate world, rational decision-making is paramount. A Stoic leader or team leverages this principle to evaluate situations objectively, ensuring that choices are driven by logic rather than fleeting emotions or biases.

Acceptance of What Is

Stoicism teaches the acceptance of the natural order of things, understanding that certain events are beyond our control. Instead of resisting or lamenting these events, Stoics learn to embrace them, finding serenity in acceptance.

"Accept the things to which fate binds you, and love the people with whom fate brings you together, but do so with all your heart." - Marcus Aurelius

Personal Context: Acceptance can lead to a profound sense of contentment in personal life, as we let go of unmet expectations and find joy in the present moment.

Business Context: Organisations face uncertainties and setbacks. Embracing the Stoic principle of acceptance allows businesses to adapt, pivot, and find opportunities even in challenging circumstances.

Focus on What's Within One's Control

Central to the Stoic mindset is the dichotomy of control. Stoics recognise that while we cannot influence external events, our reactions, judgments, and actions are within our dominion.

"We control our reasoned choice and all acts that depend on that moral will. What's not under our control are the body and any of its parts, our possessions, parents, siblings, children, or country—anything with which we might associate."
- Epictetus

Personal Context: By focusing on areas within our control, we empower ourselves to take proactive steps, cultivate resilience, and lead a purposeful life.

Business Context: In a volatile business landscape, organisations that concentrate on actionable items, fostering innovation, and employee growth, rather than external market fluctuations, position themselves for sustainable success.

In essence, the Stoic mindset is a beacon of wisdom, guiding individuals and organisations alike towards a path of reasoned judgment, acceptance, and purposeful action. By internalising these core Stoic principles, we equip ourselves to face life's vicissitudes with grace, fortitude, and clarity, ensuring excellence in both personal and professional realms.

From Philosophy to Practice: Cultivating the Stoic Mindset

While understanding the principles of Stoicism is crucial, the real transformation occurs when we move from mere comprehension to active implementation. Cultivating a Stoic mindset requires deliberate practice, introspection, and consistent effort. Let's delve into practical steps and exercises that can assist in internalising Stoic teachings and fostering a Stoic mindset in both personal and professional realms.

Morning Reflection
Start each day with a Stoic reflection or meditation. Take a moment to remind yourself of the Stoic principles, setting the tone for the day.

"Begin each day by telling yourself: Today I shall be meeting with interference, ingratitude, insolence, disloyalty, ill-will, and selfishness." - Marcus Aurelius

Personal Context: This practice cultivates mindfulness, allowing one to approach personal challenges with a Stoic perspective throughout the day.

Business Context: Leaders can share Stoic quotes or principles in morning meetings, aligning the team's mindset and encouraging Stoic values in daily operations.

Evening Review
At the end of the day, engage in introspection. Assess actions, emotions, and responses in light of Stoic teachings. Recognise areas of growth and reaffirm your commitment to Stoic principles.

"Don't allow your mind to be moulded by external circumstances; nor be enticed from the study of philosophy by other studies." - Epictetus

Personal Context: This practice encourages self-awareness and personal growth.

Business Context: Teams can have a wrap-up session, reflecting on the day's successes and areas of improvement, fostering a culture of continuous learning.

Practice the Dichotomy of Control
Whenever faced with a challenge or a decision, remind yourself of what's within your control and what's not. Focus your energy and attention on the former.

"Some things are in our control and others not." - Epictetus

Personal Context: This exercise reduces personal anxiety and empowers individuals to act proactively.

Business Context: In decision-making meetings, teams can list out controllable and uncontrollable factors, ensuring strategies are aligned with actionable items.

Engage with Stoic Texts

Regularly read and reflect on Stoic texts. Engage deeply with the teachings, making notes, and drawing parallels to current life situations.

"Books which are to be taken up again at every spare moment are most helpful." - Seneca

Personal Context: Continual engagement with Stoic texts enriches personal understanding and application.

Business Context: Organisational book clubs focusing on Stoic texts can foster collective understanding and alignment with Stoic principles.

Visualise Challenges

Engage in the Stoic practice of "premeditatio malorum" or negative visualisation. Envision potential challenges and mentally prepare for them.

"What is quite unlooked for is more crushing in its effect, and unexpectedness adds to the weight of a disaster." - Seneca

Personal Context: This exercise builds resilience and equips individuals to face potential challenges with equanimity.

Business Context: Risk assessment meetings, where potential business challenges are discussed and strategised for, ensure preparedness and proactive strategy formulation.

Incorporating these practices into daily routines, both in personal and professional contexts, ensures the cultivation of a genuine Stoic mindset. It's not a one-time effort but a continuous journey of reflection, understanding, and growth.

With consistent practice, the Stoic mindset becomes an integral part of one's worldview, guiding actions, decisions, and interactions with wisdom and clarity.

Benefits of a Stoic Mindset in Personal Life

The Stoic mindset, deeply rooted in wisdom, acceptance, and rationality, offers a plethora of benefits that touch every facet of our personal lives. Let's delve into the profound positive impacts a Stoic mindset can bestow upon our emotional landscape, relationships, and overall life purpose.

Enhanced Emotional Well-being and Resilience

Stoicism teaches us to differentiate between external events and our reactions to them. By focusing on what is within our control and accepting what isn't, we shield ourselves from the tumultuous waves of external circumstances, finding calm amidst chaos.

"You have power over your mind - not outside events. Realise this, and you will find strength." - Marcus Aurelius

This understanding translates into a heightened emotional well-being. The emotional turbulence experienced due to external setbacks is reduced, replaced with a serene acceptance and proactive approach. Resilience, a natural byproduct of this mindset, ensures that we bounce back from challenges, emerging stronger and wiser.

Improved Relationships and Interpersonal Dynamics

The Stoic principles of empathy, understanding, and justice pave the way for healthier, more fulfilling relationships. Recognising the inherent value of every individual and focusing on mutual respect and understanding, we can forge deeper connections.

"Associate with people who are likely to improve you. Welcome those who you are capable of improving." - Seneca

By adopting a Stoic mindset, conflicts are approached rationally, ego is set aside, and the focus shifts to mutual growth and understanding. Relationships, be they familial, romantic, or platonic, thrive when anchored in Stoic values of respect, understanding, and genuine affection.

Greater Clarity, Purpose, and Satisfaction in Personal Endeavours

Stoicism, with its emphasis on virtue and living in accordance with nature, provides a clear compass for personal endeavours. Goals, pursuits, and passions are aligned with one's inner values, ensuring a life of purpose and fulfilment.

"Just that you do the right thing. The rest doesn't matter." - Marcus Aurelius

With the Stoic mindset, the focus shifts from external validations to internal satisfaction. Success is redefined, no longer tied to societal benchmarks, but to personal growth, virtue, and purpose. This clarity paves the way for meaningful endeavours, bringing genuine satisfaction and contentment.

In essence, the Stoic mindset, when internalised and practiced, transforms our personal lives in profound ways. It offers a sanctuary of emotional stability, enriches our relationships, and bestows our lives with purpose and meaning. By embracing Stoicism, we not only elevate our own lives but also positively impact those around us, creating ripples of positivity, understanding, and growth.

The Stoic Mindset in Business: A Game-Changer

In the fast-paced, volatile world of business, where change is the only constant, the principles of Stoicism emerge as a beacon of stability, wisdom, and foresight. This ancient philosophy, with its emphasis on rationality, virtue, and focus on what's within one's control, finds profound relevance in modern business contexts.

Role of the Stoic Mindset in Decision-Making, Leadership, and Team Dynamics

Decision-Making: Stoicism encourages objective, clear-headed thinking, stripping away biases and emotional impulses. Decisions made from this standpoint are well-informed, balanced, and in the best interest of the organisation.

Leadership: Stoic leaders lead with empathy, vision, and integrity. They are resilient, adaptable, and always focused on the greater good, inspiring teams to strive for excellence.

Team Dynamics: Stoic principles foster a culture of mutual respect, open communication, and collective growth. Teams aligned with Stoic values are more cohesive, collaborative, and productive.

Strategies to Integrate Stoicism into Organisational Culture and Practices

Training and Workshops: Regular workshops on Stoic philosophy, its principles, and their application in business contexts. This fosters understanding and encourages employees at all levels to internalise and apply Stoic teachings.

"No person has the power to have everything they want, but it is in their power not to want what they don't have, and to cheerfully put to good use what they do have." - Seneca

Mindfulness and Reflection Practices: Incorporating daily or weekly reflection sessions, where teams can discuss challenges, learnings, and Stoic principles, ensuring continuous growth and alignment with Stoic values.

Leadership Modeling: Leaders play a pivotal role in setting the tone for organisational culture. When leaders embody and champion Stoic principles, it cascades down, shaping the very fabric of the organisation.

The Stoic mindset is not just a personal tool for growth but a game-changer in the business world. Organisations and leaders that embrace Stoicism are equipped to navigate challenges with grace, lead with vision and integrity, and foster cultures of excellence, resilience, and mutual respect. In the volatile world of business, Stoicism emerges as a timeless guide, steering organisations towards sustainable success and profound impact.

Challenges and Misconceptions

Like any philosophical doctrine with deep historical roots, Stoicism isn't immune to misconceptions and challenges. Over the centuries, it has been interpreted, reinterpreted, and sometimes misinterpreted, leading to a myriad of perceptions about what Stoicism truly represents. Furthermore, in the journey of adopting a Stoic mindset, individuals and organisations may encounter certain challenges that need addressing for a genuine understanding and implementation of its principles.

Common Misconceptions about Stoicism

Emotionless Existence: One of the most prevalent misconceptions is that Stoicism advocates for a life devoid of emotions. In reality, Stoicism doesn't ask us to suppress or negate our emotions, but rather to understand, manage, and channel them productively.

"The proper work of the mind is the exercise of choice, refusal, yearning, repulsion, preparation, purpose, and assent. What then can pollute and clog the mind's proper functioning? Nothing but its own corrupt decisions." - Epictetus

Stoicism is Pessimistic: Some perceive Stoicism as a pessimistic philosophy, focusing on suffering and misfortune. However, Stoicism is about preparedness and understanding the nature of life, not about expecting the worst.

Ancient and Outdated: Given its origins in ancient Greece and Rome, some dismiss Stoicism as outdated, not applicable to the complexities of the modern world. Yet, its core principles are timeless, offering wisdom and guidance relevant to contemporary challenges.

Challenges in Adopting a Stoic Mindset

Contrary Cultural Values: In societies that emphasise material success, external validation, or immediate gratification, adopting a Stoic mindset might seem counterintuitive. Embracing Stoic values requires a shift from predominant societal norms.

Initial Resistance to Change: As with any transformative journey, initial resistance, both internal and external, is natural. Overcoming ingrained habits of thought and behaviour can be challenging.

Misalignment with Other Belief Systems: Some might find certain Stoic principles at odds with other deeply held personal or cultural beliefs. Navigating this requires a nuanced understanding and integration of Stoic teachings.

To genuinely benefit from Stoicism, it's essential to approach it with an open mind, ready to dispel misconceptions and overcome challenges. It's about continuous learning, reflection, and application. While the path to fully internalising a Stoic mindset might have its hurdles, the rewards in terms of personal growth, emotional well-being, and professional excellence are profound and lasting.

Conclusion

The journey through the intricacies of the Stoic mindset unveils a realm of profound wisdom, timeless truths, and transformative potential. Stoicism, with its emphasis on rationality, virtue, and focus on what lies within our control, provides a robust framework for navigating the complexities of life, both personal and professional.

The Stoic mindset isn't just about understanding ancient texts or philosophies but about internalising and living these principles daily. It's about transforming our perceptions, reactions, and actions in alignment with Stoic virtues. This mindset serves as a compass, consistently guiding us towards reasoned judgment, emotional balance, and purposeful action.

As we conclude this chapter, the invitation to you, dear reader, is clear and compelling. Embrace the Stoic mindset. Delve deeper into its teachings, reflect upon its principles, and apply them in your daily life. The path might present challenges, and there might be moments of doubt, but the rewards are immeasurable. A life of clarity, contentment, resilience, and genuine fulfilment awaits.

As we set the stage for the subsequent chapters, the exploration into Stoicism continues. With each chapter, we will delve deeper, uncovering more facets of this rich philosophy and its application in various life arenas. The journey of cultivating a Stoic mindset is not just an intellectual pursuit but a transformative life experience. Embark on this journey, and discover the profound impact of Stoicism on every facet of existence.

Chapter 4
Emotional Mastery and Resilience: A Stoic Approach

In the intricate tapestry of life, emotions stand out as vibrant threads, colouring our experiences, shaping our perceptions, and influencing our decisions. These powerful forces, when harnessed correctly, can lead to profound personal well-being and professional achievements. However, left unchecked, they can also cloud judgment, impede growth, and hinder success. This duality of emotions, their potential for both upliftment and downfall, underscores the necessity for mastery over them.

Stoicism offers profound insights into the nature of emotions and the art of resilience. At its core, Stoicism teaches us that while we may not have control over external events, we possess the power to control our reactions to them. This Stoic tenet forms the foundation for emotional mastery. It's not about suppressing or negating emotions but understanding them, moderating them, and ensuring they serve us rather than enslave us.

The importance of mastering our emotions extends beyond personal well-being. In the professional realm, emotional intelligence – the ability to recognise, understand, and manage both our emotions and the emotions of others – is increasingly recognised as a key determinant of success. Leaders who exhibit emotional mastery navigate challenges with clarity, foster cohesive teams, and drive organisational growth. Similarly, teams that understand and manage their collective emotional landscape collaborate more effectively, innovate more freely, and achieve superior results.

In this chapter, we will delve deep into the Stoic approach to emotional mastery and resilience. We will explore Stoic techniques, strategies, and wisdom that can empower us to lead emotionally balanced and resilient lives, reaping the benefits in both personal and professional arenas. As we embark on this journey, let us remember that emotions, in their essence, are neither good nor bad. It's our understanding, management, and response to them that determines their impact on our lives.

The Stoic Perspective on Emotions

Emotions, in the Stoic worldview, are not adversaries to be vanquished, but rather natural aspects of the human experience. Stoicism doesn't advocate for the suppression of emotions, but rather for a deeper understanding of them, and the cultivation of a rational approach to handling them.

From the Stoic lens, emotions arise from our judgments about things we perceive. These judgments often categorise events as good or bad, beneficial or harmful. While such judgments are intrinsic to our nature, Stoics believe that they can often be mistaken or misguided, leading to powerful, sometimes turbulent emotional reactions. The Stoic practice, therefore, revolves around refining these judgments, ensuring they are based on reason, wisdom, and virtue.

Stoics differentiate between two main categories of emotions: destructive passions and natural feelings. Destructive passions, or "pathos", arise from irrational judgments and can destabilise our inner harmony. Examples include irrational fear, debilitating grief, or uncontrollable desire. On the other hand, natural feelings, such as natural affection or a rational sense of caution, are instinctual and are not seen as problematic in Stoicism. It's the irrational intensity and our reaction to these feelings that Stoics caution against.

Epictetus, one of the prominent Stoic philosophers, once remarked: *"Men are disturbed not by things, but by the view which they take of them."* This quote encapsulates the Stoic perspective on emotions, emphasising that it's not external events, but our internal judgments about them, that give rise to our emotional responses. By refining our judgments and cultivating a Stoic mindset, we can navigate the emotional landscapes of our lives with greater equanimity, clarity, and purpose.

The Four Destructive Passions

The Stoic philosophy places great emphasis on understanding and managing what they term as the "destructive passions" or "pathē". These are intense emotional reactions that arise from irrational judgments and can significantly disrupt our inner harmony. By recognising and understanding these passions, we can cultivate a sense of self-awareness and apply Stoic principles to navigate them effectively.

1. Craving (Epithumia):
At its core, epithumia is an overpowering and irrational desire for things outside our control. It's the yearning for external validations, materialistic gains, or specific outcomes that we have little to no dominion over. This unchecked craving can lead to feelings of restlessness, dissatisfaction, and can drive individuals to make impulsive decisions.
Stoic Insight: The Stoics teach us that the root of such craving is an overvaluation of externals. By recognising the transient nature of external goods and redirecting our desires towards virtue and personal growth, we can mitigate the grip of epithumia.

2. Fear (Phobos):

Phobos is the irrational fear or dread of potential future events. It's the anxiety about uncertainties, the trepidation of potential losses, or the apprehension of future challenges. Such fears can paralyse decision-making, hinder growth, and cloud judgment.

Stoic Insight: Stoicism teaches that most fears arise from giving too much value to things outside our control. By focusing on the present and grounding ourselves in the knowledge that we can handle challenges with wisdom and virtue, we can reduce the power of phobos.

3. Pleasure (Hēdonē):

Not to be confused with healthy enjoyment or contentment, hēdonē in the Stoic context refers to the irrational joy or elation over trivialities or things outside our control. It's the fleeting pleasure derived from superficial gains, often leaving individuals wanting more.

Stoic Insight: The Stoics advocate for a balanced approach to pleasure, emphasising the pursuit of eudaimonia, or flourishing, over transient delights. By seeking deeper, more meaningful joys rooted in virtue and personal growth, we can navigate the pitfalls of hēdonē.

4. Distress (Lupē):

Lupē represents the irrational sadness, grief, or anguish about current situations. It's the overwhelming sorrow over perceived losses or the dejection faced in challenging circumstances.

Stoic Insight: Stoicism reminds us that distress often arises from placing too much value on external events. By reframing challenges as opportunities for growth and recognising the impermanent nature of all things, we can diminish the impact of lupē.

In understanding these four destructive passions, we are equipped with the tools to recognise them when they arise and to apply Stoic wisdom in navigating them. By doing so, we move closer to achieving emotional mastery, ensuring that our emotions serve as guides, not masters, in our journey through life

Emotional Mastery: Techniques and Strategies

Emotional mastery is not just about understanding emotions but effectively navigating them using practical techniques. The Stoics, with their profound insights into human nature, have left us with a treasure trove of strategies that can help in mastering our emotional responses. Let's delve into some of these potent techniques:

1. Cognitive Distancing

Cognitive distancing is a powerful Stoic technique that allows us to detach from our immediate emotional reactions and view them with a sense of objectivity. Instead of getting entangled in the web of our emotions, we learn to see them as separate from our core self, almost as if we're observing them from a distance.

- **Application:** The next time a strong emotion surges, take a moment to pause. Imagine yourself stepping back and observing the emotion as an external event. Ask yourself, "Why am I feeling this way?" and "Is this emotion based on a rational judgment?"
- **Benefit:** This technique fosters a sense of calm and clarity, allowing for more reasoned responses and reducing the risk of impulsive actions.

2. Premeditation of Evils (Premeditatio Malorum)

This Stoic exercise involves mentally rehearsing potential negative outcomes. By visualising challenges or setbacks, we prepare ourselves emotionally and psychologically, thereby lessening the impact when they do occur.

- **Application:** Before embarking on a significant task or decision, take a few minutes to contemplate what could go wrong. How would you handle it? What would be your response?
- **Benefit:** By anticipating challenges, we reduce the element of surprise and can approach situations with a balanced mindset, ready with potential solutions.

3. View from Above

The 'View from Above' technique encourages us to gain a broader perspective on life. It involves visualising oneself from a cosmic viewpoint, recognising the vastness of the universe and the fleeting nature of our problems in the grand scheme of things.

- **Application:** In moments of overwhelm or distress, imagine viewing your situation from a great height, perhaps from a mountaintop or even from space. Recognise the transience of the moment and the broader tapestry of life.
- **Benefit:** This strategy fosters humility, gratitude, and a sense of interconnectedness, reducing feelings of isolation and magnifying the bigger picture.

4. Journaling

Journaling, though not exclusively Stoic, aligns perfectly with the philosophy's emphasis on self-reflection and introspection. It's a tool to articulate thoughts, process emotions, and gain clarity.

- **Application:** Dedicate a few minutes each day to jot down your experiences, emotional responses, and reflections. Over time, patterns may emerge, offering insights into triggers, reactions, and areas of growth.
- **Benefit:** Journaling cultivates self-awareness, accountability, and personal growth. It serves as a mirror to our psyche, helping us understand ourselves better and fostering emotional balance

Incorporating these Stoic techniques and strategies into our daily lives can significantly enhance our emotional mastery. By consistently practicing these methods, we not only understand our emotions better but also develop the resilience and clarity to navigate life's challenges with equanimity and wisdom.

Resilience Through Stoicism

Resilience, in essence, is the capacity to recover quickly from difficulties, to adapt and thrive in the face of adversity. It's a quality that's invaluable in both personal and professional realms, and one that the Stoics deeply understood and championed.

Stoicism, at its heart, is a philosophy of resilience. It teaches us to face the vicissitudes of life with a calm mind and a steady heart, not by denying the reality of pain and adversity, but by understanding and embracing the natural order of the world. According to Stoicism, the universe operates in a rational and orderly manner, guided by the principle of Logos. While we may not always comprehend the intricacies of this order, accepting it allows us to navigate life's challenges with a sense of purpose and understanding.

Central to Stoic resilience are the Stoic virtues, particularly courage and wisdom.

Courage: Stoics view courage not merely as physical bravery but as the moral strength to face adversity, pain, and uncertainty. It's the fortitude that enables us to confront challenges head-on, to persevere in the face of setbacks, and to uphold our principles even when it's difficult.

Wisdom: Wisdom, in the Stoic context, is the discernment to judge correctly and to act in accordance with nature. It equips us with the understanding to differentiate between what's within our control and what's not, to make informed decisions, and to navigate life's complexities with clarity.

Together, courage and wisdom form the bedrock of Stoic resilience. They empower us to face adversities with a balanced mind, to learn from challenges, and to emerge stronger and wiser.

Practical Steps to Cultivate Resilience using Stoic Principles

Regular Reflection: Engage in daily Stoic reflections to assess actions, emotions, and responses. By understanding oneself better, we can identify areas of growth and fortify our resilience.

Embrace the Dichotomy of Control: Internalise the understanding that while we can't control external events, we have full dominion over our reactions. This acceptance reduces frustration and fosters adaptability.

Seek Wisdom: Continuously educate oneself in Stoic texts and teachings. By immersing in Stoic wisdom, we can equip ourselves with the tools to handle adversities.

Community Engagement: Engage with Stoic communities, whether online forums, workshops, or local groups. Sharing experiences and learning from others can bolster resilience.

Practice Gratitude: Regularly acknowledge and be thankful for the positives in life. Gratitude shifts focus from what's lacking or challenging to what's abundant and good, fostering a positive mindset.

Engage in Challenging Situations: Actively seek out challenges or situations outside your comfort zone. Facing and overcoming these situations enhances resilience and confidence.

Resilience, as championed by Stoicism, is not a passive acceptance of fate but an active cultivation of inner strength, wisdom, and adaptability. It's about understanding the natural order, harnessing the power of Stoic virtues, and applying practical steps to face life's challenges with grace and fortitude. Through the lens of Stoicism, we come to see resilience not just as the ability to bounce back but as the capacity to grow, evolve, and flourish, no matter the circumstances.

Emotional Mastery in a Professional Context

In today's fast-paced, ever-evolving business landscape, emotional intelligence and resilience have emerged as crucial determinants of success. No longer are these qualities relegated to the realm of personal development; they are now recognised as fundamental drivers of professional growth, team cohesion, and organisational excellence.

The Significance of Emotional Intelligence and Resilience in the Workplace
Emotional Intelligence (EI), often defined as the ability to recognise, understand, and manage our emotions and those of others, is pivotal in the professional context. Employees with high EI navigate workplace dynamics with greater ease, foster collaborative environments, and lead with empathy and understanding. Furthermore, resilience, the capacity to adapt and thrive amidst challenges, ensures continuity, innovation, and sustainability in businesses, even in turbulent times.

Together, emotional intelligence and resilience form the backbone of a robust professional ecosystem. They enhance communication, facilitate effective decision-making, and promote a culture of mutual respect and growth.

Stoic Principles Guiding the Professional Arena
Stoicism, with its profound insights into human nature and emotion, offers invaluable guidance for the modern workplace:

1. **Managing Stress:** The Stoic practice of focusing on what's within our control can significantly reduce workplace stress. By accepting external factors and channeling energy towards actionable items, employees and leaders can navigate challenging scenarios with equanimity.

2. **Balanced Decision Making:** Stoic wisdom, particularly the understanding of the transient nature of external goods and the value of virtues, aids in making decisions that prioritise long-term growth and ethical considerations over short-term gains.

3. **Fostering Positive Workplace Cultures:** Stoic virtues like justice and wisdom promote a culture of fairness, mutual respect, and continuous learning. By upholding these virtues, organisations can create environments where employees feel valued, heard, and motivated.

Case Studies (Fictional): Stoic Emotional Mastery in Business

Tech Start-Up Navigates Product Failure
A promising tech start-up faced significant backlash due to a product malfunction shortly after its launch. Instead of succumbing to panic, the leadership, influenced by Stoic principles, took a step back to assess the situation objectively. They communicated transparently with

stakeholders, refocused on what was within their control, and worked diligently on rectifying the issue. Their Stoic approach not only salvaged the situation but also earned them respect and trust from their customer base.

Financial Firm Embraces Stoic Decision Making
In the volatile world of finance, a renowned firm faced a dilemma: pursue a lucrative deal with potential ethical concerns or prioritise integrity. Drawing inspiration from Stoic virtues, the firm's leadership chose the latter, reinforcing the company's commitment to ethical operations. While there was an immediate financial setback, the firm's reputation soared, leading to more sustainable and ethically-aligned opportunities in the future.

Manufacturing Company Fosters Stoic Work Culture
A global manufacturing company, facing high employee turnover and low morale, turned to Stoic philosophy to transform its workplace culture. Initiatives focused on Stoic principles of mutual respect, understanding, and continuous learning were introduced. Workshops on Stoic emotional mastery techniques were conducted. The result? Enhanced team cohesion, improved employee satisfaction, and a significant boost in productivity.

Stoic emotional mastery techniques are not just philosophical musings but actionable strategies with tangible outcomes. When integrated into the professional context, they pave the way for businesses that are not only successful but also ethical, resilient, and committed to the holistic well-being of all stakeholders.

Conclusion

As we reach the culmination of this exploration into emotional mastery and resilience through the lens of Stoicism, it's evident that the teachings of this ancient philosophy hold profound relevance in our contemporary world. Emotions, while natural and integral to the human experience, can often become overwhelming forces, steering us away from reasoned judgment and inner tranquility. Stoicism offers us a roadmap, a guide to navigating these emotional landscapes with wisdom, clarity, and purpose.

The transformative potential of emotional mastery through Stoicism is immense. By understanding, moderating, and channeling our emotions, we unlock doors to personal well-being, professional excellence, and a deeper connection with the world around us. Resilience, the ability to bounce back and thrive amidst adversities, fortified by Stoic principles, ensures that challenges become stepping stones, not stumbling blocks.

The call to action is clear: both individuals and organisations stand to gain immeasurably by integrating Stoic practices into daily life. It's not about adopting a passive or indifferent attitude but about cultivating a proactive mindset that seeks growth, understanding, and balance. By doing so, we ensure a balanced emotional terrain, ready to face the world's complexities with equanimity and resilience.

As we close this chapter, it's essential to reflect on the journey ahead. While we've explored the Stoic approach to emotions and resilience, the exploration is far from over. Subsequent chapters promise to take us further into the heart of Stoicism, revealing more facets of this rich philosophy and its myriad applications in various life arenas. With a renewed understanding of emotional mastery, we're better equipped to continue this journey, embracing the Stoic mindset and its transformative potential fully.

Step 3
Climbing with Stoic Leadership

Chapter 5
Lead Like a Stoic: Unshakeable and Wise

In the vast expanse of the business world, leadership stands as a beacon, guiding organisations towards success, innovation, and impact. Leadership, at its core, isn't just about making decisions or charting courses; it's about influencing, inspiring, and instilling a sense of purpose. The direction and quality of leadership can make or break an organisation, determining not just its financial success, but its cultural richness, ethical standing, and overall longevity.

Stoicism, with its emphasis on wisdom, virtue, and rationality, offers a unique and powerful perspective on leadership. A Stoic leader isn't swayed by fleeting trends or short-term gains; they lead with a deep-rooted sense of purpose, grounded in ethical principles and a clear vision for the future.

A Stoic approach to leadership is about more than just strategy or decision-making; it's about character. It's about leading with integrity, understanding the intrinsic value of every team member, and navigating challenges with composure and clarity. In the unpredictable seas of the business world, a Stoic leader stands firm, a steadfast anchor, guiding their team with unwavering conviction and wisdom.

Within this chapter we will explore the nuances of Stoic leadership, its transformative potential, and its application in contemporary business contexts. In a world where leadership styles come and go, Stoic leadership offers timeless insights, ensuring leaders not only achieve peak performance but also leave a lasting, positive legacy.

The Stoic Leader: Key Traits and Principles

The Stoic leader stands distinct in the panorama of leadership archetypes. While various leadership styles come with their unique sets of characteristics, the Stoic leader is distinguished by a set of traits that are deeply rooted in the ancient Stoic philosophy, yet remain strikingly relevant and vital in today's business world. Let us look at these foundational traits and principles:

Rational Decision Making

A Stoic leader understands the importance of reason and logic. They are not swayed by emotional impulses or short-term temptations. Instead, they weigh decisions carefully, considering ethical implications, long-term consequences, and the broader vision of the organisation.

"If you are distressed by anything external, the pain is not due to the thing itself, but to your estimate of it; and this you have the power to revoke at any moment."
- Marcus Aurelius

This rational approach ensures that choices made are not just beneficial for immediate gains but align with the organisation's core values and long-term objectives.

Emotional Equanimity

The business landscape is rife with challenges, uncertainties, and pressures. A Stoic leader, however, remains composed and balanced, irrespective of external circumstances. This emotional steadiness provides clarity, ensuring that challenges are navigated with wisdom rather than reactive emotion.

"Man is not worried by real problems so much as by his imagined anxieties about real problems." - Epictetus

50

By maintaining this emotional equilibrium, the Stoic leader fosters a calm and focused organisational environment, even in turbulent times.

Leading by Example

Stoicism places a significant emphasis on personal virtue and integrity. A Stoic leader embodies these principles, setting a standard for the entire team or organisation. Their actions reflect their values, ensuring trust, respect, and credibility.

"Waste no more time arguing about what a good man should be. Be one." - Marcus Aurelius

By consistently leading with virtue and integrity, the Stoic leader creates a ripple effect, encouraging a culture of ethics, responsibility, and excellence.

Empathetic Leadership

While Stoicism emphasises rationality, it does not neglect the human aspect of leadership. A Stoic leader values and understands the perspectives, feelings, and aspirations of team members. They listen actively, ensuring that each member feels valued and understood.

"Whenever you feel like criticising anyone, just remember that all the people in this world haven't had the advantages that you've had." - Epictetus

This empathy fosters mutual respect, open communication, and a cohesive team environment where members feel empowered and aligned with the organisation's vision.

In essence, the Stoic leader is a harmonious blend of reason and empathy, principle and flexibility, vision and understanding. These key traits and principles not only ensure effective leadership but also create a legacy of positive influence, ethical standing, and organisational excellence.

Stoicism and Strategic Vision

Strategic vision is the North Star for any organisation, guiding its trajectory, influencing its decisions, and shaping its future. For Stoic leaders, this strategic vision isn't just about setting goals or forecasting trends; it's a holistic approach rooted in the core tenets of Stoicism—foresight, planning, and adaptability.

The Stoic Emphasis on Foresight
Foresight, for Stoics, is the ability to perceive the deeper currents beneath the surface waves of immediate circumstances. It's about understanding the broader picture, anticipating potential challenges, and foreseeing opportunities.

"First say to yourself what you would be; and then do what you have to do." - Epictetus

A Stoic leader, with this foresight, can discern not only the immediate implications of decisions but also their long-term impact on the organisation and its stakeholders.

The Value of Planning
While Stoicism teaches acceptance of things beyond our control, it also emphasises the importance of diligent planning for what is within our grasp. Planning, in the Stoic context, is a proactive approach, ensuring that the organisation is prepared, come what may.

"If a man knows not to which port he sails, no wind is favourable." - Seneca

This quote embodies the Stoic wisdom that, while we must accept what we cannot control, we must also have a clear plan and direction for the areas where we do have influence. It's a reminder that purposeful planning is essential to navigate through life's uncertainties effectively. Strategic planning, under Stoic leadership, is comprehensive, ethical, and aligned with the organisation's core values. It's not about reacting to the market but shaping the market with innovative, principled strategies.

Adaptability: The Stoic Response to Change

In the ever-evolving landscape of business, change is the only constant. Stoicism, with its teachings on acceptance and adaptability, equips leaders to navigate this change with grace and agility.

"We cannot choose our external circumstances, but we can always choose how we respond to them." - Epictetus

For a Stoic leader, adaptability isn't just about pivoting strategies but about maintaining a clear vision amidst the flux. It's about ensuring that, even in the face of unforeseen challenges, the organisation's core principles remain unshakeable.

Navigating Challenges with a Clear, Unwavering Vision

Challenges, in the Stoic worldview, are not obstacles but opportunities—for growth, learning, and reaffirmation of purpose. A Stoic leader, when confronted with challenges, remains anchored in the organisation's vision.

"Obstacles are not opposing you, but merely guiding you on your path." - Marcus Aurelius

This unwavering commitment to the vision ensures that even in turbulent times, the organisation remains on course, its values intact, and its purpose clear.

Stoic leadership, when applied to strategic vision, results in an approach that is both visionary and grounded, both ambitious and ethical. It ensures that organisations, under the guidance of Stoic leaders, are not just chasing success but are crafting a legacy of positive impact, resilience, and enduring excellence.

Building and Leading Stoic Teams

In the intricate tapestry of organisational success, teams are the threads that weave together its very fabric. Effective, cohesive, and motivated teams are pivotal to achieving organisational goals. But what distinguishes an ordinary team from a Stoic one? It's the ethos, the culture, and the principles they abide by. Let's delve into the nuances of building and leading teams through the Stoic lens.

Cultivating a Team Culture Rooted in Stoic Principles
The foundation of a Stoic team lies in its principles - principles of integrity, virtue, and rationality. A Stoic leader, in their quest to build such a team, emphasises the importance of these values, ensuring that they permeate every aspect of team dynamics.

"Men are not disturbed by things, but by the view which they take of them." - Epictetus

This principled approach results in teams that are not just performance-oriented but are also ethical, responsible, and aligned with the broader organisational vision.

Encouraging Mutual Respect, Open Communication, and Collective Growth
A Stoic team thrives in an environment of mutual respect. Every member, irrespective of their role or experience, is valued for their unique contributions.

Open communication is encouraged, fostering an environment where ideas are shared freely, feedback is constructive, and innovation is celebrated.

The Stoic leader ensures that the team's growth is collective. Individual achievements are celebrated, but the emphasis is always on collective success, mutual support, and collaborative achievement.

Addressing and Resolving Conflicts with Wisdom and Fairness

Conflicts, disagreements, and challenges are inevitable in any team setting. However, in a Stoic team, these are approached with a unique perspective.

Rather than viewing conflicts as disruptions, they are seen as opportunities for growth, understanding, and further alignment.

"When another blames you or hates you, or when men say anything injurious about you, approach their poor souls, penetrate within, and see what kind of men they are."
- Marcus Aurelius

A Stoic leader addresses conflicts with wisdom, ensuring that resolutions are fair, just, and in alignment with Stoic virtues. They promote dialogue, understanding, and mutual respect, ensuring that conflicts lead to deeper bonds rather than divisions.

In essence, building and leading Stoic teams is a journey of intention, principle, and purpose. Under the guidance of a Stoic leader, teams transform into cohesive units that are not just focused on goals but are also deeply rooted in values, ethics, and mutual respect. Such teams don't just achieve success; they set benchmarks for excellence, integrity, and collaborative achievement.

Challenges in Stoic Leadership

Every leadership style, no matter how effective or principled, faces its share of challenges, and Stoic leadership is no exception. As organisations attempt to integrate Stoic principles into their leadership frameworks, they might encounter resistance, misconceptions, and challenges that can deter their journey. Understanding these challenges and devising strategies to overcome them is pivotal for the successful adoption of Stoic leadership.

Addressing Potential Misconceptions
One of the primary challenges faced by Stoic leaders is the myriad of misconceptions surrounding Stoicism. Some view it as a philosophy of emotional suppression, while others mistake its teachings of acceptance as passive resignation.

"It's not events that upset us, but our judgments about events." - Epictetus

Effective Stoic leaders address these misconceptions head-on, clarifying that Stoicism is not about negating emotions but understanding and channeling them effectively. It's not about passive acceptance but proactive action within the realm of what's under one's control.

Resistance to Stoic Leadership Principles
Change, especially at the leadership level, can be met with resistance. Introducing Stoic principles might be seen as a departure from traditional leadership models, leading to skepticism or apprehension.

"It is not death that a man should fear, but he should fear never beginning to live."
- Marcus Aurelius

Stoic leaders navigate this resistance by leading by example, demonstrating the effectiveness and integrity of Stoic leadership in action. They engage in open dialogues, addressing concerns, sharing success stories, and emphasising the long-term benefits of Stoic leadership.

Strategies to Overcome Challenges

Education and Awareness: Conducting workshops, seminars, and training sessions on Stoic philosophy and its relevance in leadership. This helps in dispelling myths and provides a clear understanding of Stoic principles.

Mentorship Programs: Pairing potential Stoic leaders with mentors who have successfully integrated Stoicism into their leadership styles. This provides hands-on learning and real-time feedback.

Feedback Mechanisms: Establishing channels for continuous feedback, allowing team members to share their experiences, concerns, and suggestions regarding Stoic leadership. This ensures that the leadership style remains dynamic and responsive to the needs of the organisation.

Consistent Communication: Regularly communicating the vision, purpose, and values of Stoic leadership ensures that the entire organisation is aligned and moving in the same direction.

While challenges are inherent in the adoption of any new leadership style, they are not insurmountable. With clarity, conviction, and a commitment to Stoic principles, leaders can navigate these challenges effectively, ensuring that Stoic leadership becomes an integral and transformative force within their organisations.

Case Studies (Fictional): Successful Stoic Leaders in Business

The proof of the pudding is in the eating. While the principles of Stoic leadership might resonate on paper, it's their application in the real world that truly attests to their effectiveness. Across the business landscape, there have been numerous leaders who, knowingly or unknowingly, have embodied Stoic principles, driving their organisations to unparalleled success.

Leader A: The Visionary Entrepreneur

Background: Leader A founded a tech startup in the early 2000s. Amidst the tumultuous landscape of the tech bubble and its subsequent burst, this entrepreneur demonstrated remarkable resilience and foresight.

Stoic Principles in Action: Despite facing financial challenges and market skepticism, Leader A remained unwavering in his vision. Embodying the Stoic principle of focusing on what's within one's control, he concentrated on product development and team morale, rather than external market fluctuations.

"Seek not the good in external things; seek it in yourselves." - Epictetus

Outcome: Today, his company stands as one of the tech giants, testament to his Stoic resilience, vision, and adaptability.

Leader B: The Ethical CEO

Background: Taking the helm of a multinational corporation, Leader B was faced with the challenge of navigating ethical quandaries, especially in overseas markets with differing business practices.

Stoic Principles in Action: Rather than succumbing to potentially lucrative but unethical business practices, Leader B emphasised integrity and virtue. She believed in the Stoic principle that true success is not just about profit, but about honour and righteousness.

"The soul becomes dyed with the colour of its thoughts." - Marcus Aurelius

Outcome: The company not only saw financial growth under her leadership but also became a benchmark for ethical business practices globally.

Leader C: The Innovator and People's Champion:

Background: Leader C spearheaded a consumer goods company known for its innovative products.

Stoic Principles in Action: More than just product innovation, Leader C was renowned for his people-centric leadership. Embodying the Stoic principles of empathy and mutual respect, he established an organisational culture where every voice was valued, and every idea had merit.

"Whenever you are about to find fault with someone, ask yourself the following question: What fault of mine most nearly resembles the one I am about to criticise?"
- Marcus Aurelius

Outcome: Under his leadership, the company not only launched market-leading products but also boasted one of the highest employee satisfaction rates in the industry.

These case studies illuminate the transformative potential of Stoic leadership. Whether it's resilience in the face of adversity, unwavering ethical commitment, or a deep-seated respect for team members, Stoic principles have proven to be a guiding light for leaders across various industries. Their successes underscore the timeless relevance of Stoicism and its profound impact on leadership and organisational excellence.

Integrating Stoic Leadership into Organisational Culture

A leader's philosophy is not just personal; it can shape the ethos of an entire organisation. As leaders begin to embrace Stoic principles, there arises an imperative to integrate these principles at every level, ensuring that the entire organisation operates with the same Stoic-inspired ethos. Doing so requires strategic planning, commitment, and continuous reinforcement. Here's how Stoic leadership can be seamlessly integrated into an organisational culture.

Organisational Vision and Mission Rooted in Stoic Principles

For Stoic leadership to permeate an organisation, its very vision and mission need to echo Stoic values. This could mean emphasising long-term sustainable growth over short-term gains or prioritising ethical considerations in all business decisions.

"Our life is what our thoughts make it." - Marcus Aurelius

Leaders must ensure that organisational goals and KPIs align with Stoic principles, creating a roadmap that is both ambitious and ethical.

Practical Steps and Initiatives

Stoic Leadership Workshops: Regular workshops where teams are introduced to Stoic principles, their relevance in the business context, and practical exercises to internalise them.

Stoic Reflection Sessions: Monthly or quarterly sessions where teams reflect on their decisions, challenges, and learnings in the light of Stoic teachings.

Stoic Mentorship Programs: Pairing emerging leaders with seasoned Stoic leaders, allowing for hands-on guidance, real-world application, and continuous feedback.

Training Programs

Comprehensive training programs can be devised that not only introduce Stoic philosophy but delve deep into its application in day-to-day business scenarios. These could cover topics like Stoic decision-making, conflict resolution, and strategic planning.

"It is not what happens to you, but how you react to it that matters." - Epictetus

Such training programs can be made mandatory for leadership roles, ensuring that as leaders climb the organisational ladder, they are well-versed in Stoic principles.

Leadership Retreats Focused on Stoic Teachings

Organising annual or biennial leadership retreats with a focus on Stoicism. These retreats can combine theoretical sessions with practical exercises, allowing leaders to immerse themselves in Stoic teachings.

Nature retreats, mirroring the Stoic practice of connecting with nature and understanding one's place in the larger cosmos, can be particularly effective.

"Look back over the past, with its changing empires that rose and fell, and you can foresee the future too." - Marcus Aurelius

These retreats also offer leaders a chance to disconnect from daily operations, reflect on their leadership style, and return with renewed clarity and commitment to Stoic principles.

Continuous Reinforcement

For Stoic leadership to truly take root, it requires continuous reinforcement. Regular communication from top leadership emphasising Stoic values, celebrating Stoic successes, and reflecting on areas of improvement can ensure that Stoic leadership remains at the forefront.

Integrating Stoic leadership into organisational culture is a journey that requires vision, commitment, and consistency. However, the rewards are manifold: organisations that operate on Stoic principles are not only successful but also ethical, resilient, and deeply connected to a larger purpose. They stand as beacons of excellence, demonstrating that success and virtue can, indeed, go hand in hand.

Conclusion

Leadership is more than just guiding a team or an organisation to success; it's about leaving a lasting legacy, shaping the future, and making a meaningful impact. As we journeyed through the intricacies of Stoic leadership, it's evident that the age-old wisdom of Stoicism offers a beacon for modern leaders, illuminating a path that's both virtuous and effective.

The transformative potential of Stoic leadership is undeniable. By emphasising rationality, virtue, and a deep understanding of the human psyche, Stoic leaders not only drive their organisations to success but also ensure that this success is sustainable, ethical, and aligned with the greater good. They demonstrate that in the volatile landscape of the business world, it's possible to remain unshakeable, wise, and principled.

Stoic leadership is not about endless deliberations or getting lost in philosophical intricacies. It's about action, embodiment, and living the principles we believe in. For leaders looking to make a lasting impact, to lead teams that are motivated, ethical, and high-performing, and to create organisations that stand as pillars of excellence and integrity, the Stoic way offers invaluable insights.

Embrace Stoic leadership. Immerse yourself in its teachings, reflect on its principles, and embody them in your leadership journey. The challenges of the business world are many, but armed with the wisdom of Stoicism, leaders are equipped to navigate them with grace, wisdom, and unwavering resolve.

In the chapters that follow, we will delve deeper into the practical applications of Stoicism in various business case studies. But the foundation is set. Stoic leadership is not just a philosophical ideal; it's a tangible, actionable blueprint for success. And the journey to 'Stoicism at the Summit' is one every leader can embark upon, ensuring peak performance, impactful leadership, and a legacy that stands the test of time.

Chapter 6
Building and Leading Stoic Teams: Strategies for Sustainable Success

In the ever-evolving world of business, an organisation's success is often determined not just by its strategies or products but by the people who drive its vision forward. A cohesive, motivated, and aligned team can be the difference between a flourishing organisation and one that struggles to find its footing. Team dynamics, which encompass the interactions, relationships, and collective output of a group, play a pivotal role in shaping the trajectory of an organisation.

Stoicism holds profound relevance in today's corporate landscape. Stoicism, with its emphasis on rationality, virtue, and control over one's own actions and responses, offers invaluable insights into building and leading successful teams. When teams operate with a Stoic mindset, they are better equipped to navigate challenges, foster positive interpersonal relationships, and work towards a common goal with clarity and purpose.

Imagine a team where members practice emotional equanimity, reacting to successes and setbacks with a balanced perspective. Envision a group where individuals prioritise collective success over personal gain, driven by a shared vision and mutual respect. Think of a team that thrives on open communication, values feedback, and is resilient in the face of adversity. This is the potential of a Stoic team.

Within this chapter we will explore the practicalities of building such teams, the leadership strategies that promote Stoic values, and the transformative impact of Stoicism on team dynamics. From recruitment strategies to conflict resolution, Stoic principles offer a roadmap to team excellence, ensuring that organisations don't just reach the summit but thrive there.

The Stoic Foundation for Teams

Stoicism, at its heart, is a philosophy centred on understanding the nature of life and our role within it. While often discussed in the context of individual growth and self-mastery, its principles are incredibly relevant to the collective dynamics of teams. To truly grasp how Stoicism can be the bedrock of high-performing teams, we first need to delve into the core Stoic principles that resonate with team building.

The Dichotomy of Control
One of the foundational tenets of Stoicism is understanding what is within our control and what isn't. For teams, this translates into focusing on collective actions, strategies, and responses, while accepting external factors that cannot be changed. It promotes proactive problem-solving and reduces unnecessary stressors, leading to a more harmonious and productive team environment.

Virtue as the Highest Good
Stoics believe that living a life of virtue is the ultimate goal. In team contexts, this means prioritising ethical actions, honesty, and integrity in all dealings. When a team operates with virtue at its core, trust is fostered, and collaborations become more effective.

Rationality and Objectivity
Stoicism teaches the importance of rational thought and objective judgment. Teams that embody this principle are better equipped to make informed decisions, evaluate situations without bias, and approach challenges with a clear, logical mindset.

Acceptance and Resilience

Stoics emphasise accepting the natural order of things and facing adversity with resilience. For teams, this means navigating challenges with a positive, can-do attitude and viewing setbacks as opportunities for growth and learning.

Cosmopolitanism

The Stoic belief in seeing all humans as part of a larger, interconnected whole encourages inclusivity and diversity in teams. It fosters a culture where all team members, irrespective of their background, are valued and heard.

Now, having understood these principles, how do they shape Stoic team dynamics? A lot of it boils down to mutual respect, understanding, and shared goals.

Mutual Respect

Drawing from the Stoic principle of cosmopolitanism, mutual respect in teams ensures that every member's contribution is valued. It diminishes ego clashes and fosters a positive team culture where members support and uplift each other.

Understanding

Stoic teams prioritise open communication and empathy. By practicing emotional equanimity and objective judgment, team members are better equipped to understand each other's perspectives, leading to more collaborative and effective problem-solving.

Shared Goals

A Stoic team is aligned in its vision and purpose. By focusing on what's within their control and prioritising virtue, such teams work cohesively towards common objectives, ensuring that individual actions contribute to the collective good.

In essence, the Stoic foundation for teams is about creating a harmonious, effective, and ethical team environment. It's about recognising the collective strength of diverse individuals working towards a shared vision, underpinned by Stoic wisdom and values. Such teams not only achieve their goals but do so with integrity, resilience, and mutual respect, standing as shining examples of what Stoicism can achieve in the modern business landscape.

Building a Stoic Team

The foundation of any successful team is its members. Building a team that embodies Stoic values and principles requires a strategic approach from the very beginning – from recruitment to onboarding, and continuous training and development.

Recruitment
The hiring process is the first step in shaping a Stoic team. While skills, experience, and technical expertise are undoubtedly essential, the Stoic approach to recruitment goes beyond these tangible qualifications:

Character Assessment: Stoicism places a high value on virtue and character. During the hiring process, it's essential to assess a candidate's integrity, honesty, and ethical stance. This can be achieved through behavioural interview questions, references, and real-world scenarios that test a candidate's character in action.

Resilience Evaluation: Stoic teams are resilient, able to navigate challenges with a balanced mindset. Potential team members should demonstrate their ability to handle setbacks, adapt to changing circumstances, and maintain emotional equanimity in the face of adversity.

Alignment with Stoic Values: It's crucial to ensure that potential hires resonate with Stoic principles. This doesn't mean they need to be scholars of Stoicism, but they should showcase values like rationality, acceptance, and a focus on what's within their control.

Onboarding

Once a new member joins the team, the onboarding process plays a pivotal role in integrating them into the Stoic team culture.

Introduction to Stoic Values: New team members should be familiarised with the Stoic principles that guide the team's actions and decisions. This can be done through workshops, reading materials, or discussions.

Setting Expectations: Clearly communicate what's expected in terms of behaviour, collaboration, and decision-making. Emphasise the importance of mutual respect, open communication, and a collective focus on shared goals.

Mentorship Programs: Pairing new hires with seasoned team members who embody Stoic values can be a practical way to ensure a smooth transition and integration into the team's Stoic culture.

Training and Development

To maintain and strengthen the Stoic team culture, continuous training and development are paramount.

Regular Workshops: Organise workshops that delve deeper into Stoic teachings, exploring their relevance in modern business scenarios and team dynamics.

Feedback Mechanisms: Implement systems where team members can give and receive feedback, promoting self-awareness and continuous improvement in alignment with Stoic principles.

Growth Opportunities: Ensure that team members have opportunities to grow, both professionally and personally. Encourage them to reflect on their actions, decisions, and interactions, fostering a culture of continuous learning and alignment with Stoic values.

Building a Stoic team is a strategic and ongoing process. It's about ensuring that from the moment a potential team member is considered, through their journey within the organisation, Stoic principles guide their path. Such teams stand out in their cohesion, resilience, and effectiveness, proving that Stoicism, though ancient, holds timeless wisdom for today's business world.

Leading a Stoic Team

In the realm of leadership, where actions ripple across teams and organisations, Stoicism provides a solid anchor, grounding leaders in virtues that stand the test of time and challenges. The ancient teachings of Stoicism, while rooted in personal introspection, offer profound insights into the dynamics of leading teams effectively.

"Leadership is not about being in charge. It is about taking care of those in your charge."
– Seneca

This statement by Seneca captures the essence of Stoic leadership. Instead of wielding authority as a tool of power, Stoic leaders use it as a means of service, ensuring that every team member is supported, understood, and empowered.

The Role of the Stoic Leader
Guidance: Stoic leaders serve as the team's compass, offering direction and clarity. By ensuring alignment with

organisational and Stoic values, they pave the way for collective success.

Motivation: Tapping into the unique strengths and aspirations of each team member, Stoic leaders motivate from a place of genuine understanding and appreciation. They recognise that individuals are motivated by purpose and alignment with a greater good.

Support: Ever-present and approachable, Stoic leaders are the pillars of support for their teams. They understand the nuances of human emotions and are adept at providing the right resources, encouragement, and guidance when needed.

"Begin at once to live, and count each separate day as a separate life." – Seneca

Emphasising shared responsibility, open communication, and mutual respect is at the core of Stoic leadership:

Shared Responsibility: Every team member, under Stoic leadership, is an integral part of the collective mission. There's an emphasis on collective ownership, where successes are celebrated together, and challenges are navigated as a united front.

Open Communication: Stoic leaders champion a culture of honesty and transparency. They create safe spaces for open dialogues, ensuring every voice is heard and valued.

Mutual Respect: In a Stoic-led team, respect isn't a function of hierarchy but a testament to character and contribution. Every team member, irrespective of their role, is treated with dignity and appreciation.

Case Studies (Fictional): Showcasing Successful Stoic Team Leadership in Action

Case Study 1: Tech Titan's Transformation

Background

In the heart of Silicon Valley, the tech company "NexaTech" was once synonymous with high-stress, burnout, and fierce internal competition. Founded in the late 90s, the company quickly grew to dominate the tech scene, known for its groundbreaking innovations. However, behind the scenes, the culture was toxic. Employee turnover was high, inter-departmental collaboration was almost non-existent, and the pressure to outperform was intense.

The Turning Point

Enter Alex Ramirez, appointed as the new CEO in 2015. Ramirez, an avid reader and philosopher, had recently discovered Stoicism. Intrigued by its principles of rationality, acceptance, and focus on what's within one's control, he began to integrate Stoic teachings into his personal life, experiencing profound shifts in his perspective and well-being.

Recognising the potential for transformation at NexaTech, Ramirez began a mission: to reshape the company's culture using Stoic principles.

Initiatives and Changes

Open Forums: Ramirez introduced monthly open forums where employees at all levels could voice their concerns, ideas, and feedback without fear of retribution. He actively participated, listening and often quoting Stoic philosophers like Marcus Aurelius and Epictetus to emphasise the value of open dialogue and mutual respect.

Mindfulness and Reflection Sessions: Understanding the Stoic emphasis on introspection, NexaTech started offering weekly mindfulness and reflection sessions. These sessions became a space for employees to pause, reflect, and realign with their core values.

Collaborative Projects: Breaking the silos, Ramirez encouraged inter-departmental projects. He often said, "We're in this together, like the Stoics believed, interconnected and interdependent."

Leadership Workshops: Ramirez recognised that for a culture shift to be sustainable, the leadership team needed to be on board. He organised Stoicism-based leadership workshops, emphasising virtues like wisdom, courage, and justice.

The Results
Over the next few years, NexaTech saw a remarkable shift.

Employee Satisfaction: Annual surveys showed a significant uptick in employee satisfaction and morale.

Innovation: With barriers broken down, collaboration soared, leading to breakthrough innovations and faster project completions.

Financial Growth: As a result of increased employee retention, collaboration, and innovation, NexaTech's financial performance improved considerably.

Industry Recognition: NexaTech's transformation didn't go unnoticed. They started receiving accolades for their positive work culture, with many in the industry looking to them as a model for organisational health.

Conclusion
Ramirez's leadership, inspired by Stoic principles, showcased that success in the business world isn't just about profits and

market share. It's about creating environments where individuals can thrive, collaborate, and innovate. NexaTech's transformation stands as a testament to the power of Stoic leadership in action, offering insights and inspiration for leaders across industries.

Case Study 2: The Small Business Success

Background
In the bustling streets of Brooklyn, "Café Lumina" stood out not just for its aromatic coffees but also for its unique business ethos. Founded by Isabella Mireles in 2010, this quaint café had more to offer than met the eye. Operating in a competitive market, with several cafes in close proximity, Café Lumina was a small business facing the typical challenges: limited funding, tight margins, and fierce competition.

Isabella's Stoic Journey
Isabella's introduction to Stoicism came during a challenging phase. Facing financial constraints and considering closing her café, she stumbled upon a book on Stoicism in a local library. As she delved into the teachings of Seneca, Marcus Aurelius, and Epictetus, she found solace and inspiration. The Stoic teachings about facing adversities with equanimity and focusing on one's actions resonated deeply with her. Determined to infuse her business with these newly discovered Stoic principles, Isabella began a transformative journey for Café Lumina.

Stoic Principles in Action
Value-driven Recruitment: Isabella started hiring staff based not just on skills, but on character and alignment with the café's Stoic values. She often quoted, *"Character matters, for it drives our actions and shapes our interactions."*

Client Interactions: Customer service at Café Lumina wasn't just about politeness; it was about genuine connection, understanding, and service. Isabella trained her staff to approach interactions with empathy and authenticity, often reflecting on the Stoic principle of seeing the inherent value in every individual.

Facing Challenges: In the volatile world of small businesses, challenges were aplenty. However, with her Stoic mindset, Isabella approached every challenge as an opportunity to learn and grow. She instilled in her team the Stoic belief of viewing obstacles as the way forward.

Community Engagement: Understanding the Stoic emphasis on community and interconnectedness, Café Lumina started hosting monthly community events, fostering connections, and giving back to the local community.

The Impact
Café Lumina's Stoic-inspired approach bore fruit.

Loyal Customer Base: The café quickly built a loyal customer base, with many patrons drawn to its warm, authentic atmosphere and value-driven approach.

Employee Satisfaction: Turnover rates dropped as employees felt valued, understood, and aligned with the café's mission.

Financial Stability: While Café Lumina may not have become a millionaire venture, it achieved steady profitability and financial stability, a significant achievement in the challenging small business landscape.

Local Recognition: Café Lumina became a local favourite, receiving accolades from community organisations and local media for its unique approach and community engagement.

Conclusion

Isabella's journey with Café Lumina stands as a testament to the transformative power of Stoic principles, even in the realm of small business. Her story showcases that with the right values, mindset, and determination, even small ventures can make a significant impact, creating ripples of positive change in their communities.

Case Study 3: The Non-Profit Champion

Background

"HopeSprings Foundation" was a modest non-profit based in Atlanta, focusing on providing educational resources and support to underprivileged children. Founded in 2005, the organisation faced the typical challenges of a non-profit: limited funding, dependency on volunteers, and the immense responsibility of making a real difference in the community.

The Stoic Leadership of Marcus Greene

In 2012, Marcus Greene, a well-read advocate of Stoic philosophy, took the helm as the new director of HopeSprings. Marcus believed in the transformative power of education and was deeply passionate about the foundation's mission. His leadership style, deeply influenced by Stoic principles, was about to usher in a new era for the organisation.

Stoic Leadership in Action

Navigating Challenges: Marcus often quoted Epictetus, saying, *"It's not what happens to you, but how you react to it that matters."* When faced with funding challenges or administrative hurdles, Marcus approached them with calmness, clarity, and strategic thinking, always focusing on what was within his control.

Rallying Volunteers: Recognising that the heart of the foundation was its volunteers, Marcus emphasised the Stoic principle of duty and service. He organised regular workshops, sharing Stoic wisdom, and highlighting the intrinsic value of selfless service. This not only boosted volunteer morale but also attracted more individuals to the foundation's cause.

Community Engagement: Marcus believed in the Stoic principle of the interconnectedness of all beings. Under his leadership, HopeSprings started community engagement programs, collaborating with local businesses, schools, and other organisations. This not only expanded the foundation's reach but also deepened its impact.

Resource Management: Marcus often reflected on the Stoic teaching of making the best use of available resources. He implemented cost-effective strategies, ensuring that the maximum portion of donations directly benefited the children.

The Results
Under Marcus's Stoic leadership, HopeSprings Foundation witnessed:

Expanded Outreach: The foundation's programs reached more children than ever before, with improved quality and impact.

Increased Donations: With transparent operations, impactful initiatives, and Marcus's genuine Stoic-inspired approach, the foundation saw a significant increase in donations.

Volunteer Growth: The number of volunteers doubled in just a few years, with many citing the organisation's Stoic values as a key attraction.

Community Recognition: HopeSprings became a beacon of hope in the community, receiving recognition and awards for its exemplary work and impact.

Conclusion

The success of HopeSprings Foundation under Marcus Greene's leadership underscores the immense potential of Stoic principles in guiding organisations, especially non-profits. It's a testament to the idea that when leadership is rooted in timeless virtues and wisdom, it can navigate challenges, inspire teams, and create lasting positive change in communities.

Leading like a Stoic is not just about personal mastery but about elevating the collective potential of a team. It's about recognising the interconnectedness of success, where every individual's growth, well-being, and contribution play a pivotal role. As we journey further into the nuances of Stoic leadership in business, we'll discover its transformative power, offering a roadmap to sustained success and harmonious team dynamics.

Stoic Strategies for Team Challenges

Teams, being a microcosm of human relationships, naturally encounter challenges. However, Stoic principles offer a guiding light, turning these challenges into opportunities for growth, cohesion, and progress.

Navigating Conflicts with Wisdom and Fairness

Conflicts are an inevitable part of team dynamics. Yet, Stoic philosophy teaches us to approach disagreements not as adversarial confrontations, but as opportunities for growth and mutual understanding. As Seneca once stated, *"We are more often frightened than hurt; and we suffer more from imagination than from reality."* In team conflicts, it's essential to separate perceived slights from genuine issues, addressing the root causes with openness and empathy. By encouraging dialogue and seeking common ground, Stoic leaders can transform conflicts into bridges, fostering deeper connections and mutual respect within the team.

Addressing Team Burnout, Stress, and Challenges
In today's fast-paced work environment, burnout and stress are prevalent challenges. Stoicism, with its emphasis on inner tranquility and understanding the nature of things, offers solace. Marcus Aurelius reminded us, *"Look within. Within is the fountain of good, and it will ever bubble up, if you will ever dig."* Leaders should create environments where team members feel safe to express their concerns, ensuring that workloads are manageable and that there's a balance between work and rest. By recognising the signs of burnout early and addressing them with Stoic understanding and care, leaders can ensure that their teams remain motivated, engaged, and resilient.

Adapting to Change and Uncertainty with a Stoic Mindset
Change is the only constant, and in the business world, it often comes with a fair share of uncertainty. However, Stoicism teaches acceptance and adaptability. When faced with change, whether it's a shift in market dynamics, organisational restructuring, or the introduction of new technologies, Stoic leaders guide their teams with a steady hand. They emphasise the importance of focusing on what's within one's control, adapting with flexibility, and viewing change as an opportunity rather than a threat.

The challenges faced by teams are multifaceted, but Stoic principles provide a robust framework to navigate them. By infusing team dynamics with Stoic wisdom, leaders can foster environments of trust, resilience, and adaptability, ensuring that challenges are not just overcome but turned into stepping stones for greater success.

Cultivating a Stoic Team Culture

A team's culture is its lifeblood, shaping interactions, decisions, and overall performance. Infusing this culture with

Stoic principles can lead to a harmonious, resilient, and highly effective team dynamic.

Daily Practices and Rituals that Reinforce Stoic Values
Every action, no matter how small, can serve as a reminder of Stoic values. Leaders can introduce daily team rituals that emphasise mindfulness, gratitude, and duty. Starting meetings with a Stoic quote or a moment of reflection can set the tone for the day. One might consider the words of Musonius Rufus: *"Practice and exercise in the things which one uses daily is by far the most important and necessary thing in life."* By instilling such practices, teams can be constantly reminded of the Stoic principles of rationality, duty, and mutual respect.

Encouraging Individual Reflection and Collective Growth
Stoicism places great emphasis on self-awareness and personal growth. Leaders can foster a culture where team members are encouraged to reflect on their actions, decisions, and interactions. By setting aside time for individual reflection and group discussions, teams can explore their collective strengths and areas of improvement. As Seneca mentioned, *"As long as you live, keep learning how to live."* By promoting a culture of continuous learning and reflection, leaders ensure that the team remains adaptable, cohesive, and aligned with Stoic values.

The Role of Feedback and Continuous Improvement in a Stoic Team Culture
Feedback is a crucial component of growth. However, in a Stoic team culture, feedback is approached not as criticism but as an opportunity for growth. Both giving and receiving feedback are done with kindness, clarity, and the intention of mutual benefit. Hierocles, a Stoic philosopher, emphasised the importance of our connections, saying, *"We should feel toward our fellow human beings as parts of ourselves."* In this spirit, feedback sessions become collaborative endeavours, where the focus is on collective growth and continuous

improvement. Leaders play a pivotal role in setting the tone for these sessions, ensuring they are constructive, solution-oriented, and rooted in Stoic principles of empathy and understanding.

Cultivating a Stoic team culture is a continuous journey, requiring intention, effort, and a deep understanding of Stoic principles. However, the rewards are manifold. Teams that embrace Stoicism become more cohesive, resilient, and effective, navigating challenges with grace and achieving remarkable success. Through daily practices, continuous reflection, and a culture of feedback, Stoic principles become the guiding light, leading teams to unparalleled heights of excellence.

Benefits of a Stoic Team

While Stoicism might seem like an ancient, abstract philosophy, when applied to modern team dynamics, its principles have tangible and lasting benefits. A team grounded in Stoicism is not just equipped to face challenges but is also poised to thrive in various facets of organisational life.

Analysing the Long-Term Advantages of Teams Rooted in Stoic Principles

Stoic teams, by their very nature, look beyond the immediate and transient. They focus on long-term goals, sustainable practices, and the broader good of the organisation and its stakeholders. This long-term vision, as emphasised by the Stoic philosopher Seneca, is paramount: "*It's not because things are difficult that we dare not venture. It's because we dare not venture that they are difficult.*" Stoic teams dare to venture, to innovate, and to push boundaries, all the while ensuring that their actions align with ethical and sustainable practices.

Impact on Productivity

One of the primary benefits of a Stoic team is enhanced productivity. With a culture of mutual respect, open communication, and a focus on what's within one's control, team members are empowered to perform at their best. The Stoic principle of focusing on the present moment, as Epictetus mentioned, *"There is only one way to happiness and that is to cease worrying about things which are beyond the power of our will,"* ensures that team members are fully engaged in their tasks, leading to improved efficiency and output.

Innovation

Stoic teams are not just productive; they are also innovative. By embracing the Stoic value of continuous learning and by fostering an environment where new ideas are celebrated, organisations can become hubs of creativity and innovation. As Marcus Aurelius stated, *"The universe is transformation; life is opinion."* Teams that embrace change and value diverse opinions are better equipped to innovate and stay ahead of the curve.

Employee Satisfaction

A team culture rooted in Stoic values is also a key driver of employee satisfaction. When team members feel valued, understood, and empowered, their job satisfaction and overall well-being improve. This not only reduces turnover but also attracts top talent who align with the organisation's Stoic values.

Overall Organisational Success

The benefits of a Stoic team, when compounded, lead to overall organisational success. Teams that are productive, innovative, and satisfied play a pivotal role in driving growth, improving the bottom line, and enhancing the organisation's reputation in the market.

The benefits of a Stoic team are manifold and far-reaching. By embracing Stoic principles, organisations can unlock unparalleled potential, ensuring not just short-term gains but also long-term, sustainable success. In the modern business landscape, where challenges are myriad and competition fierce, Stoic teams stand out, leading the way with wisdom, virtue, and unwavering resilience.

Challenges and Mitigations

The journey to integrating Stoicism within team dynamics, while transformative, isn't without its challenges. Resistance, misconceptions, and implementation hurdles can emerge along the way. However, with understanding, strategy, and persistence, these challenges can be transformed into stepping stones, further solidifying the team's commitment to Stoic principles.

Addressing Potential Misconceptions or Resistance to Stoic Team Principles

One of the primary challenges faced in adopting Stoicism is the potential misconceptions surrounding it. Some may view Stoicism as advocating for emotional suppression, or as an outdated philosophy with no relevance in the modern workplace. Chrysippus, an influential Stoic philosopher, once stated, *"The fact that the door is closed is not a reason for failing to arrive. Instead, we should break it down if it does not open."* It's essential to break down these misconceptions by offering clarity on what Stoicism truly advocates: rationality, acceptance, and focus on what's controllable.

Resistance can also emerge from team members who might be set in their ways or wary of any new approach. To overcome resistance, it's crucial to highlight the richness that Stoic values bring, emphasising the personal and collective benefits they offer.

Strategies and Best Practices for Successful Integration
Education and Training: Begin with comprehensive workshops and training sessions on Stoic philosophy, its relevance, and its practical application in the workplace. As Epictetus pointed out, *"Only the educated are free."* Equip teams with knowledge, and freedom to embrace Stoicism will follow.

Open Dialogue: Encourage open discussions where team members can voice their concerns, ask questions, and share experiences related to Stoic practices. This fosters understanding and dispels any lingering doubts.

Lead by Example: Leadership plays a pivotal role. When leaders embody Stoic values and principles in their actions and decisions, it sets a powerful precedent for the entire team.

Introduce Stoic Rituals: Incorporate Stoic practices into daily routines, like beginning meetings with a moment of Stoic reflection or having monthly Stoic book discussions.

Feedback and Continuous Improvement: Regularly solicit feedback on the implementation of Stoic practices. Understand what's working and where adjustments are needed. Remember the Stoic emphasis on adaptability and use feedback as a tool for continuous improvement.

While challenges in integrating Stoicism within teams are inevitable, they are not insurmountable. With the right strategies, a commitment to education, and continuous engagement, Stoic principles can become the bedrock of team culture. The rewards – in terms of productivity, team cohesion, and overall well-being – are well worth the effort, leading teams to not just navigate challenges but to truly thrive in the face of them.

Conclusion

The Stoic philosophy, while ancient in its origin, holds profound relevance in our modern world, particularly within the realm of team dynamics. Its principles resonate deeply, offering teams a compass by which to navigate the complexities of organisational life.

Reflecting on the Transformative Potential of Stoic Teams
At the heart of Stoicism lies the pursuit of virtue, rationality, and a deep understanding of one's place within the broader cosmos. Teams that embed these principles into their core function with a heightened sense of purpose and unity. As the Stoic philosopher Musonius Rufus aptly stated, *"We should not practice to speak well, but to live well."* Stoic teams do just that – they live well, fostering environments where mutual respect, open communication, and collective growth are the norm.

In the volatile landscape of modern business, where uncertainties abound and challenges are a constant, Stoic teams emerge as beacons of stability and resilience. They are equipped not just to weather storms, but to harness challenges as opportunities for growth and learning. As the renowned Stoic, Hierocles, once said, *"Conduct me, Jove, and you, O Destiny, wherever your decrees have fixed my station."* Stoic teams, grounded in acceptance and proactive endeavour, excel irrespective of external circumstances.

A Call to Action

To leaders, managers, and organisational visionaries: The call to action is clear. Embrace the Stoic philosophy at the team level. Invest in the training, practices, and cultural shifts that make this possible. The dividends – in terms of team cohesion, productivity, and overall organisational health – are significant.

The ancient Stoics believed in the interconnectedness of all beings, an idea captured by Marcus Aurelius when he said, *"What is harmful to the hive is harmful to the bee."* By nurturing teams that are harmonious, balanced, and guided by Stoic principles, organisations not only benefit the individual members but also the broader 'hive' – the entire organisation and its stakeholders.

As we look to the future, the vision is one of Stoic teams leading the way, embodying ancient wisdom in contemporary settings, and setting new standards for excellence in teamwork and leadership. The journey towards building and leading Stoic teams is not just a strategic choice; it's a call to a higher, more enlightened way of collective functioning. Embrace it, champion it, and watch as it transforms your organisational landscape.

Step 4
Strategies and Execution

Chapter 7
Stoic Strategies for Sustainable Business Growth

The business landscape is ever-evolving, filled with challenges, uncertainties, and opportunities. In this dynamic environment, what principles can guide a business towards sustainable growth? Stoicism, an ancient philosophy that, despite its age, has never been more relevant to the world of business.

The Intersection of Stoicism and Strategic Business Growth

Stoicism is not merely about individual well-being or personal philosophy; its principles extend far beyond, touching every facet of human endeavour, including business. As Seneca once said, *"Luck is what happens when preparation meets opportunity."* In the context of business, this 'preparation' can be seen as the strategies we formulate, and 'opportunity' represents the market scenarios we encounter. Stoicism teaches us that while we cannot always control external opportunities, we can control our preparation, our strategies, and our reactions.

Strategic business growth, therefore, aligns naturally with Stoic principles. It's about seeing the bigger picture, making decisions not just for immediate gain but for long-term sustainability. It's about understanding the external environment, yet not being swayed by every market fluctuation, instead focusing on building a strong, resilient core that can withstand challenges and capitalise on opportunities.

How Stoic Principles Uniquely Position Businesses for Sustainable Success

Stoicism offers businesses a roadmap to sustainable success by emphasising several core tenets. Firstly, the Stoic emphasis on virtue aligns seamlessly with ethical business practices. As Epictetus elegantly put it, *"Wealth consists not in having great possessions, but in having few wants."* In a business context, this speaks to the importance of sustainable growth over unchecked expansion, of ethical practices over short-term gains.

Moreover, Stoicism teaches acceptance of what is outside our control and urges us to focus our energy on areas where we can make a real impact. For businesses, this translates into adaptability, a willingness to pivot when necessary, and a focus on continuous improvement and innovation. As Marcus Aurelius stated, *"The obstacle is the way."* Challenges, from a Stoic business perspective, are not setbacks but opportunities to learn, innovate, and grow stronger.

Stoic philosophy and strategic business growth are two sides of the same coin. Together, they offer a path to businesses that is not just about financial success, but about building organisations that are resilient, ethical, and geared for long-term, sustainable success. As we go deeper into this chapter, we will uncover the many ways in which Stoic principles can be the guiding light for businesses aiming for the summit of their potential.

The Stoic Approach to Business Strategy

In the realm of business, where change is the only constant, Stoic philosophy offers a timeless approach to strategy. At its core, Stoicism emphasises rationality, adaptability, and a commitment to ethical action. These principles, when applied to business strategy, offer a blueprint for sustainable success in an unpredictable market landscape.

Understanding the Stoic Emphasis on Long-Term Vision, Adaptability, and Ethical Decision-Making

Stoic philosophy is grounded in the understanding of nature's order and our role within it. It teaches acceptance of things we cannot change and encourages proactive engagement with what we can influence. In the words of Epictetus, *"First, say to yourself what you would be; and then do what you have to do."* Translated into business parlance, this means establishing a clear, long-term vision for the company and then setting in motion the strategies and actions needed to achieve it.

However, in the pursuit of this vision, adaptability becomes crucial. Markets evolve, technologies advance, and consumer preferences shift. A Stoic business strategy is not rigid; it is flexible, always ready to adapt to the ever-changing external environment. As Seneca reminds us, *"Every new beginning comes from some other beginning's end."* In the unpredictable world of business, the ability to let go of outdated strategies and embrace new, innovative approaches is essential.

Central to the Stoic approach is the unwavering commitment to ethical decision-making. Business strategies should not merely aim for profit but should consider the broader impact on society, the environment, and stakeholders. Marcus Aurelius, the Roman Emperor and Stoic philosopher, once stated, *"Never let the future disturb you. You will meet it, if you have to, with the same weapons of reason which today arm you against the present."* This Stoic wisdom reminds businesses to equip themselves with ethical and rational strategies, ensuring sustainable success regardless of future challenges.

The Role of Stoic Virtues in Shaping Business Strategies

Stoic virtues – wisdom, courage, justice, and temperance – play a pivotal role in shaping business strategies. Wisdom guides informed and rational decision-making, ensuring that businesses choose the best path forward. Courage empowers businesses to take calculated risks, innovate, and venture into uncharted territories. Justice ensures that strategies are ethical, fair, and beneficial for all stakeholders. And temperance, with its emphasis on moderation, ensures that growth is sustainable and resources are used judiciously.

Incorporating these virtues into business strategies ensures a holistic approach that considers not just profits, but also the well-being of employees, customers, communities, and the environment. In essence, the Stoic approach to business strategy offers a balanced, ethical, and sustainable path forward. By grounding strategies in Stoic virtues and principles, businesses are better equipped to navigate challenges and seize opportunities, ensuring lasting success in the ever-evolving world of commerce.

Informed Decision Making

Decisions, both big and small, shape the trajectory of a business. From hiring to product development, from marketing campaigns to partnerships, every decision has consequences. In this labyrinth of choices, Stoic philosophy serves as a compass, guiding businesses towards decisions that are not only profitable but also ethical and sustainable.
Using Stoicism to Guide Decisions: Balancing Intuition with Rationality
One of the cornerstones of Stoicism is the emphasis on rational thought. Stoics believe that humans possess a unique capacity for reason, which should be honed and utilised. In the realm of business, this translates to a rigorous analytical approach to decision-making, where every choice is evaluated based on evidence, logic, and long-term implications.

However, Stoicism also acknowledges the value of intuition. As Epictetus asserted, *"It is not events that disturb people, it is their judgements concerning them."* In business, this suggests that while data and analysis are crucial, there's also a place for instinct, for that gut feeling which often arises from experience and deep understanding. The art lies in balancing this intuition with rationality, ensuring that decisions are both informed and instinctual.

Embracing the Stoic Emphasis on Ethics and the Common Good in Business Decisions

Beyond the mechanics of decision-making lies the realm of ethics. Stoic philosophy places a profound emphasis on virtue and the common good. In business terms, this means that decisions shouldn't just be about bottom lines but should also consider broader impacts. Every business decision has ripple effects – on employees, on customers, on communities, and on the environment. Stoicism urges businesses to be acutely aware of these ripples.

Seneca's wisdom resonates profoundly here: *"We are not given complete lives but only the raw material and the duty of shaping it."* Businesses have the raw material – resources, talent, and opportunities. The choices they make shape this material into the legacy they leave behind.

Another Stoic, Hierocles, emphasised the interconnectedness of all individuals, likening society to a series of concentric circles with oneself at the centre. In a business context, this signifies the interconnectedness of an organisation with its stakeholders and the broader community. Decisions should, therefore, be made with this interconnectedness in mind, ensuring benefits not just for the business but for the broader ecosystem it operates within.

Stoicism offers businesses a roadmap to informed and ethical decision-making. By integrating Stoic principles, businesses can navigate the complexities of the commercial world with clarity, ethics, and a commitment to the greater good. The decisions made under this guiding light are bound to be ones that stand the test of time, ensuring sustainable success and a legacy of positive impact.

Stoic Risk Management

In the volatile and unpredictable landscape of business, risk is an ever-present companion. While conventional business strategies often approach risk with trepidation, Stoic philosophy offers a refreshingly different perspective. For Stoics, risk and challenges aren't just obstacles to be feared but are opportunities for growth, learning, and fortification.

The Stoic View of Challenges as Opportunities
At the heart of Stoic philosophy is the belief that challenges are an inherent part of life. Rather than bemoaning adversity, Stoics see it as a crucible for character development. As Marcus Aurelius wisely observed, *"The obstacle is the way."* Translated into the business context, this means that challenges, setbacks, and risks are not just hurdles to overcome but are opportunities to innovate, adapt, and emerge stronger.

Seneca, another Stoic luminary, stated, *"Difficulties strengthen the mind, as labour does the body."* For businesses, this reinforces the idea that navigating risks and challenges can lead to resilience, sharpening the organisation's strategic acumen and adaptability.

Strategies for Proactive Risk Assessment and Mitigation Grounded in Stoic Principles
Anticipatory Thinking: Drawing from the Stoic practice of Premeditatio Malorum (premeditation of evils), businesses can actively anticipate potential risks. By mentally rehearsing

worst-case scenarios, they can be better prepared and less emotionally reactive when challenges arise.

Focus on What's Controllable: One of the foundational Stoic teachings is to focus on what's within our control and accept what isn't. In risk management, this translates to concentrating efforts on actionable mitigation strategies while developing resilience towards uncontrollable external factors.

Ethical Considerations: Stoicism places a high value on virtue and ethics. In risk management, this means always considering the ethical implications of business decisions and actions. As Epictetus reminded us, *"What decides whether a sum of money is good? The money is not going to tell you; it must be the faculty that makes use of such impressions – reason."* Businesses should evaluate risks not just in terms of financial impact but also in terms of ethical and societal repercussions.

Continuous Learning and Reflection: Stoics believe in the value of reflection and learning from experiences. After navigating a risk or challenge, businesses should take the time to reflect, learn from the experience, and refine their strategies moving forward.

In essence, Stoic risk management is about proactive anticipation, ethical decision-making, and seeing challenges as opportunities for growth. By embracing these Stoic principles, businesses can navigate the uncertain terrains of the commercial world with confidence, wisdom, and a forward-looking vision, ensuring not just survival but sustainable success.

Growth Through Stoic Innovation

Innovation is the lifeblood of business growth. As markets evolve and consumer preferences change, businesses must continually reinvent themselves to stay relevant and competitive. But how does one foster a culture of innovation? The Stoic philosophy, with its emphasis on rationality, adaptability, and learning from challenges, provides a roadmap.

Encouraging Innovation by Fostering a Stoic Work Culture

Stoicism teaches us to approach life with an open mind, to question the status quo, and to seek knowledge relentlessly. This ethos can be translated into a work culture that values creativity, encourages out-of-the-box thinking, and celebrates diverse perspectives. As the Stoic philosopher Seneca said, *"It's a rough road that leads to the heights of greatness."* In the context of business innovation, this means that the path to groundbreaking ideas and solutions often involves challenging conventions and venturing into the unknown.

Creating a Stoic work culture involves:

Open Dialogue: Encouraging team members to voice their opinions, ideas, and concerns freely.

Continuous Learning: Promoting a culture of continuous learning, where team members are encouraged to upskill, explore new domains, and bring fresh insights to the table.

Acceptance of Diversity: Recognising that diverse teams bring diverse ideas. Embracing diversity in thought, background, and experience can be a catalyst for innovation.

The Stoic Approach to Failure: Learning, Iterating, and Growing

Failure is often stigmatised in business contexts, but from a Stoic perspective, failure is not a dead-end but a detour. It's an opportunity to learn, iterate, and grow stronger. Marcus Aurelius aptly remarked, *"Our actions may be impeded... but there can be no impeding our intentions or our dispositions. Because we can accommodate and adapt. The mind adapts and converts to its own purposes the obstacle to our acting.* " This Stoic view of adaptability in the face of impediments aligns perfectly with the iterative process of innovation.

In the world of innovation, not every idea will be a home run. Some might falter, while others might face unforeseen challenges. However, the Stoic approach encourages businesses to:

Analyse Failures Objectively: Instead of assigning blame, dissect what went wrong, and why.

Iterate Based on Feedback: Use the insights gained from failures to refine and improve ideas.

Embrace Failure as a Stepping Stone: As the Stoic philosopher Epictetus noted, *"Difficulties are things that show a person what they are."* In the realm of business innovation, difficulties can reveal gaps, areas of improvement, and new avenues to explore.

Growth through Stoic innovation is about fostering a culture that values open dialogue, learning, and adaptability. It's about seeing failures not as setbacks but as opportunities for growth. In the ever-evolving landscape of business, this Stoic approach to innovation ensures not just growth, but sustainable and ethical growth that stands the test of time.

Sustainable Business Relationships

In the intricate web of the business world, relationships form the crucial threads that bind the entire tapestry together. From clients to suppliers, from partners to employees, sustainable business relationships act as the foundation upon which lasting success is built. Stoicism, with its emphasis on ethics, rationality, and virtue, provides invaluable insights into cultivating and nurturing these relationships.

Building and Maintaining Relationships with Stakeholders
At the heart of Stoicism lies the principle of living in accordance with nature and reason. In the context of business, this translates to relationships that are genuine, transparent, and rooted in mutual respect. As the Stoic philosopher Epictetus wisely observed, *"Men are disturbed not by things, but by the views which they take of them."* When businesses view stakeholders not just as transactional entities but as partners in a shared journey, the dynamics of the relationship shift towards trust and collaboration.

Stoic values to embed in stakeholder relationships include:

Trust: The cornerstone of any relationship. Delivering on promises and being transparent in dealings fosters trust.

Integrity: Acting with honesty, even when it's not the easiest path. As Marcus Aurelius noted, *"Never esteem anything as of advantage to you that will make you break your word or lose your self-respect."*

Mutual Respect: Recognising the value and perspective of every stakeholder, regardless of their role or stature.

Strategies for Conflict Resolution and Collaboration
Conflicts are inevitable in business, but the Stoic approach to conflict resolution is rooted in understanding, empathy, and seeking common ground. Many conflicts arise from misunderstandings or misaligned perceptions. Stoicism teaches us to step back, assess the situation rationally, and address the root cause rather than the symptoms.

Effective Stoic strategies for conflict resolution and collaboration include:

Active Listening: Ensuring that all parties feel heard and understood can defuse tensions and pave the way for productive discussions.

Seeking Win-Win Solutions: Instead of a zero-sum approach, seeking outcomes that benefit all parties involved.

Empathy and Perspective-taking: Understanding the concerns and motivations of others, as reflected in the Stoic practice of putting oneself in another's shoes.

Sustainable business relationships, when approached with Stoic principles, become more than mere transactions. They evolve into partnerships characterised by trust, collaboration, and mutual growth. By integrating Stoic values into business dealings, organisations can ensure that their relationships are not just profitable but also ethical, meaningful, and enduring.

Stoic Financial Strategies

In the complex realm of business finance, the turbulent ebb and flow of market forces, shifting economic landscapes, and the unpredictable nature of financial trends can often lead to reactionary decision-making. Stoicism, however, offers a refreshing perspective on financial strategy, emphasising steadiness, foresight, and ethical considerations.

Financial Planning Inspired by Stoic Principles
Stoicism teaches us to focus on what is within our control and to accept what isn't. When applied to financial planning, this means a disciplined approach, immune to the capriciousness of external market pressures.

Key Stoic-inspired financial planning principles include:

Prudence: Avoiding unnecessary risks and ensuring that every financial decision is well-thought-out.

Moderation: Preventing overextension, whether in investments, expansions, or acquisitions.

Focus on the Long Term: Looking beyond immediate gains to ensure the long-term financial health of the business.

Sustainability, Ethical Investments, and Long-term Financial Health
Stoicism, at its core, is about living in alignment with nature and virtue. In financial terms, this translates to sustainable and ethical financial practices. As Marcus Aurelius wisely stated, *"What is not good for the swarm is not good for the bee."* Businesses must recognise that financial decisions have broader implications, affecting not just the company's bottom line but also the community, the environment, and society at large.

Essential Stoic financial strategies include:

Sustainable Investments: Prioritising projects and investments that have long-term viability and are environmentally friendly.

Ethical Financial Practices: Ensuring transparency in financial dealings, avoiding unethical practices, and prioritising investments that align with the company's values.

Long-term Financial Health: Emphasising steady growth, maintaining adequate financial reserves, and avoiding short-term financial decisions that might jeopardise the company's long-term stability.

Stoic financial strategies offer businesses a roadmap to not only achieve financial success but to do so in a manner that is ethical, sustainable, and in harmony with the broader world. By integrating Stoic principles into financial decision-making, businesses can ensure that their growth is not just profitable but also principled and enduring.

Operational Excellence Through Stoicism

In the vast machinery of a business, operations form the backbone. Ensuring that this backbone is strong, agile, and efficient is critical for the overall health and success of an organisation. Stoicism, with its emphasis on rationality, simplicity, and focus, provides invaluable insights into achieving operational excellence.

Streamlining Operations with Stoicism

The Stoic philosophy places a high value on simplicity and purpose. Seneca, one of the great Stoic thinkers, once said, *"True happiness is to enjoy the present, without anxious dependence upon the future."* In the context of operations, this can be understood as focusing on the present processes, ensuring they are as streamlined and effective as possible without being overly entangled in complexities.

Key Stoic-inspired operational principles include:

Simplicity: Eliminating unnecessary steps, redundancies, and complexities in operational processes.

Efficiency: Ensuring that every process adds value and is aligned with the organisation's goals.

Purpose: Each operational process should have a clear purpose, ensuring that resources are utilised for maximum impact.

The Role of Stoic Leaders in Driving Operational Excellence

A Stoic leader's role in operations is pivotal. Their clarity of thought, unwavering focus, and ethical stance can shape the operational strategies of an organisation. Two hallmarks of Stoic leadership are having a clear vision and taking decisive action.

For Stoic leaders, operational excellence is not just about processes but also about people. It involves:

Empowering Teams: Providing teams with the tools, training, and autonomy they need to excel.

Continuous Improvement: Embracing a mindset of continuous learning and improvement, always seeking better ways to achieve objectives.

Ethical Operations: Ensuring that operations are conducted ethically, transparently, and with respect for all stakeholders involved.

Operational excellence, when approached through the lens of Stoicism, goes beyond mere efficiency. It becomes a holistic strategy that encompasses processes, people, and purpose. By embracing Stoic principles in operations, businesses can achieve a level of excellence that is sustainable, ethical, and truly impactful.

Case Studies (Fictional): Companies Excelling with Stoic Strategies

Across the business landscape, from fledgling startups to established industry giants, the timeless wisdom of Stoicism has found its application in myriad ways. The following case studies shed light on companies that have seamlessly integrated Stoic principles into their growth strategies, reaping not just financial rewards but also forging a path of sustainable and ethical business practices.

1. The Eco-Friendly Startup's Stoic Turnaround

In the bustling city of San Francisco, nestled among tech giants and innovative disruptors, lay 'GreenSustain', a fledgling eco-friendly startup with a vision to revolutionise sustainable living. Founded by a group of passionate environmentalists, the company initially made waves with its innovative products and eco-conscious mission. However, as the initial euphoria faded, they were met with the harsh realities of running a business. Financial constraints began to tighten, and the startup's future seemed uncertain.

Drawing from the Stoic philosophy, the leadership reflected on the words of Marcus Aurelius: "*Very little is needed to make a happy life; it is all within yourself, in your way of thinking.*" Recognising the power of perspective, they embarked on a journey of introspection. Instead of seeking external validations and aggressive expansions, they pivoted their strategy towards internal growth.

The company began streamlining its operations, cutting down on wasteful expenditures and redundancies. They fostered a company culture that encouraged innovation from within, leading to the development of new, cost-effective, and eco-friendly products. 'GreenSustain' also prioritised genuine engagement with its community. They organised workshops, webinars, and community clean-up events, forging a strong bond with their customer base. This not only created a loyal customer community but also attracted like-minded investors who believed in their vision.

Their Stoic-inspired approach focused on authentic growth, valuing ethical principles over fleeting profit. Over time, 'GreenSustain' not only recovered from its financial challenges but also emerged as a trusted brand in the eco-friendly market. Their journey was a testament to the power of Stoic principles: that by looking inward, understanding one's true values, and focusing on genuine, ethical growth, businesses can not only survive challenges but also thrive in the face of them.

2. The Retail Giant's Ethical Overhaul

In the heart of New York's bustling commercial district stood 'RetailMax', a retail behemoth with hundreds of stores nationwide. Known for its vast product range and competitive prices, it was a household name. However, behind the glitz and glamour of its success lay a series of ethical concerns. Allegations of unfair labour practices, environmentally unsound operations, and questionable sourcing strategies started emerging, casting shadows on its glowing reputation.

As the pressures mounted, the company's board had a significant decision to make. They could continue their current trajectory, ignoring the murmurs and focusing solely on profit margins, or they could pivot, embracing a more ethical, Stoic-inspired approach to business.

In a move that surprised many industry experts, 'RetailMax' chose the latter. The board, inspired by the Stoic saying from Seneca, *"Not for school but for life we learn,"* decided that it was time to make meaningful, long-lasting changes. They believed that while immediate profits might take a hit, the long-term goodwill and ethical alignment would ensure the company's sustainable growth.

They embarked on a massive overhaul of their supply chain, ensuring fair labour practices and sourcing products from ethical, sustainable sources. They invested in renewable energy for their stores and distribution centres, significantly reducing their carbon footprint. Employee welfare programs were introduced, ensuring better working conditions, fair wages, and growth opportunities for their staff.

But perhaps the most Stoic-inspired change was their shift in marketing strategy. Instead of aggressive sales tactics, 'RetailMax' started promoting mindful consumption. They introduced educational campaigns for consumers, highlighting the importance of ethical buying choices and their impact on the world.

This overhaul wasn't without its challenges. Initial costs soared, and there was skepticism from various quarters. However, as time went on, the wisdom of their Stoic approach became evident. Consumer trust in 'RetailMax' grew exponentially. The brand, once associated with fast fashion and consumerism, transformed into a symbol of ethical retailing.

Their journey demonstrated that even in the cut-throat world of retail, Stoic principles of ethics, long-term vision, and genuine commitment to the greater good could pave the way for sustainable success.

3. The Tech Pioneer's Focus on Sustainable Innovation

Amid the fast-paced world of technology, where innovation and disruption are the orders of the day, there lies 'Tech-Futura', a tech company known for its innovative solutions. However, as rapid advancements began to shape the industry, 'Tech-Futura' found itself at a crossroads. Speedy innovation was often at odds with sustainable and ethical practices, leading to a potential compromise on their core values.

Inspired by Epictetus's words, *"First say to yourself what you would be; and then do what you have to do,"* 'Tech-Futura' embarked on a mission to redefine innovation. They realised that for them to remain industry leaders and true pioneers, they had to ensure that their innovations were not only technologically advanced but also ethically grounded and environmentally sustainable.

To this end, 'Tech-Futura' started investing in green technologies, aiming to reduce their carbon footprint. They launched initiatives to minimise electronic waste, offering customers incentives to return old devices for recycling. Their product design teams were tasked with creating devices that were not only cutting-edge but also made from sustainable materials, ensuring a longer lifecycle and reduced environmental impact.

Beyond the products, 'Tech-Futura' also took a Stoic approach to its business operations. Recognising the importance of the collective over the individual, they prioritised team collaboration and open communication, ensuring that every team member, irrespective of their role, had a voice in the innovation process. They also launched mentorship programs, emphasising continuous learning and growth, aligning with the Stoic principle of self-improvement.

The company's Stoic-inspired shift was not without challenges. It required significant initial investments and a departure from the traditional tech mindset. However, the results spoke for themselves. 'Tech-Futura' not only solidified its position as a technological leader but also set new industry standards for sustainable and ethical innovation.

Their story serves as a testament to the power of Stoic philosophy: that real success lies not just in achieving goals, but in ensuring those achievements are grounded in values, ethics, and a larger vision for the betterment of society.

In essence, these case studies highlight the transformative potential of Stoic strategies in the business realm. When companies, regardless of their size or industry, embed Stoic values at the heart of their strategies, they pave the way for growth that's not just financially rewarding but also ethically grounded and sustainably achieved.

Conclusion

As we draw this chapter to a close, the profound influence of Stoicism on sustainable business growth becomes undeniably evident. In a world where short-term gains often eclipse long-term vision, the Stoic principles offer guidance, ensuring that businesses not only thrive but do so with integrity, purpose, and a commitment to the greater good.

Marcus Aurelius once remarked, "*What we do now echoes in eternity.*" This sentiment resonates deeply in the realm of business. The choices made today, the strategies employed, and the values upheld will undoubtedly shape the legacy of any organisation. By adopting Stoic strategies, businesses are not just securing their success for today but are laying the foundation for an enduring legacy that stands the test of time.

Seneca's wisdom also offers a guiding light: "*It's not that we have a short time to live, but that we waste much of it.*" Time, in the world of business, is a valuable asset. How companies use that time, the strategies they employ, and the principles they uphold will determine their trajectory. A Stoic approach ensures that businesses make the most of their time, driving growth while staying true to their core values.

Looking ahead, one can envision a future where businesses worldwide are influenced by Stoic principles. A world where companies prioritise ethical decision-making over quick profits, where sustainable growth is favoured over rapid expansion, and where every stakeholder, from the employees to the customers, is valued and respected. As Epictetus aptly put it, "*The key is to keep company only with people who uplift you, whose presence calls forth your best.*" In the future, may businesses be those uplifting entities, drawing out the best in society and leading the way towards a brighter, Stoic-inspired world.

Chapter 8
Making Informed and Ethical Decisions: a Stoic Approach

Every business, irrespective of size or industry, constantly teeters on the precipice of decisions. These decisions, big or small, have the potential to shape the company's trajectory, influence stakeholders, and leave an indelible mark on society. More than just the economic implications, decisions in the business realm bear an ethical weight. This ethical dimension isn't just a philosophical consideration; it's a tangible factor that can determine long-term sustainability, brand reputation, and stakeholder trust.

Stoicism encourages us to approach decisions with reason, foresight, and a deep sense of responsibility. Rather than being swayed by transient emotions or short-term gains, Stoicism nudges us towards a more holistic, ethically grounded decision-making process.

Seneca opined, *"We are more often frightened than hurt; and we suffer more from imagination than from reality."* In the context of business, this insight underscores the importance of separating perceived threats or opportunities from genuine ones, leading to decisions grounded in reality rather than speculative fears or desires.

Within this chapter we'll explore how Stoic principles can guide businesses towards making decisions that are not only informed and strategic but also ethically sound and beneficial for the broader community.

Understanding Stoic Wisdom in Decisions

Central to Stoic philosophy is the pursuit of wisdom. But this wisdom isn't just an abstract concept; it's a practical tool that guides everyday choices, both in personal life and in the complex landscape of business. At its core, Stoic wisdom urges us to differentiate between things we can control (our actions, intentions, and judgments) and things we can't (external events, outcomes, and others' judgments). This discernment becomes the foundation for ethical and informed decisions.

One of the Stoic virtues that resonates deeply with decision-making is 'phronesis' or practical wisdom. This virtue emphasises the need for decisions to be rooted in both knowledge and moral virtue. As the Stoic philosopher Epictetus declared, *"It is impossible for a man to learn what he thinks he already knows."* In the realm of business, this insight speaks to the need for continuous learning, humility, and openness to new perspectives, ensuring that decisions are both informed and adaptive.

Another significant Stoic tenet is the focus on the common good. Stoics believe that as social beings, our decisions should not be solely self-centred; they should also consider the broader community's well-being. In a business context, this translates to ethical decisions that account for stakeholders at all levels—from employees and customers to society at large. Musonius Rufus, a lesser-known but profound Stoic teacher, once said, *"We must keep in mind the whole of which we are a part."* This sentiment reminds business leaders that their decisions have ripples, impacting the larger business ecosystem.

Lastly, the Stoic emphasis on temperance—a balance and moderation in all things—guides businesses away from extreme or impulsive decisions. Instead, it encourages thoughtful deliberation, considering all facets of a situation.

As the Stoic Seneca profoundly noted, *"For many men, the acquisition of wealth does not end their troubles, it only changes them."* This insight is particularly relevant for businesses tempted by rapid expansion or aggressive strategies without considering long-term implications.

In drawing these parallels between Stoic virtues and business decision-making, it becomes evident that Stoic wisdom offers a robust and ethically grounded framework. A framework that not only ensures the sustainability of business ventures but also their alignment with broader societal values and well-being.

The Stoic Decision Matrix

In the diverse and often volatile world of business, having a consistent framework to evaluate decisions can be an invaluable asset. Enter the Stoic Decision Matrix, a tool rooted in ancient Stoic teachings but remarkably relevant to modern-day challenges. By integrating the four cardinal Stoic virtues—wisdom, courage, justice, and temperance—this matrix provides a holistic perspective on decision-making, ensuring that choices are both ethically sound and strategically astute.

The foundation of this matrix lies in **wisdom**, which in a Stoic context refers to the ability to discern what's truly valuable and what's ephemeral. As Marcus Aurelius, the Stoic emperor, once reflected, *"If it is not right, do not do it; if it is not true, do not say it."* In a business scenario, this virtue encourages leaders to sift through noise, focus on core objectives, and prioritise long-term value over short-term gains.

Next comes **courage**. But Stoic courage isn't just about facing physical adversities; it's about moral courage—the willingness to act rightly even when it's challenging or unpopular. For businesses, this might mean making tough choices that uphold company values, even if they aren't the most profitable. As the Stoic philosopher Cato stated, *"An honourable death is better than a dishonourable life."* In the corporate world, this could translate to the idea that maintaining integrity is more crucial than transient success.

Justice is the third pillar of the matrix. To the Stoics, justice meant treating each individual with fairness and kindness, recognising our shared humanity. In business terms, this virtue guides leaders to ensure equitable practices, valuing each stakeholder's contributions, and fostering an inclusive work environment. The words of Hierocles, a Stoic philosopher, resonate deeply here: *"Let our relations with one another be harmonious, and let us not be angry with our brothers or view them with suspicion."* It's a call for unity and mutual respect, which are integral for cohesive and productive teams.

Finally, temperance encourages moderation and self-control, ensuring that decisions aren't driven by excess or impulsivity. For businesses, this virtue emphasises sustainable growth, resource optimisation, and avoiding the pitfalls of overextension. As Chrysippus, an influential Stoic thinker, remarked, *"The right reason to pursue anything is because it's the natural and logical thing to do."* This perspective encourages businesses to adopt strategies that are not only profitable but also sustainable and grounded in reality.

By employing the Stoic Decision Matrix, businesses can navigate complex challenges with a balanced and ethical lens, ensuring that their trajectory aligns not just with profit margins but also with the core Stoic virtues that champion a harmonious and just society.

Ethical Profitability: A Stoic Perspective

In the realm of business, there exists a longstanding myth: that ethics and profitability are at odds, that one must often be sacrificed to attain the other. However, from a Stoic perspective, this dichotomy is a false one. The Stoic teachings emphasise the interconnectedness of our actions and their consequences, suggesting that true, sustainable profitability can only be attained when it aligns with ethical principles.

Seneca stated, *"We are not given complete control."* In the context of business, this means that while we can strive for profitability, it should not be pursued at the expense of ethical considerations, as these external gains can be fleeting. Instead, the focus should be on what we can control: our intentions, actions, and the moral compass that guides our decisions.

Another foundational Stoic belief is the idea that true wealth isn't just material but is also found in the richness of one's character. For businesses, this translates to the understanding that chasing after endless profits without a moral foundation can lead to a void, where the more one gains materially, the more one might lose ethically.

Musonius Rufus, often considered Rome's foremost Stoic, emphasised the importance of right action over mere outcomes. He declared, *"It is not the man who has too little that is poor, but the one who hankers after more."* This Stoic insight challenges businesses to redefine success, recognising that the relentless pursuit of profits without ethical considerations is a hollow victory. True success, from a Stoic perspective, encompasses both financial health and moral integrity.

In the modern business landscape, where consumers are becoming increasingly conscious of corporate ethics and social responsibility, aligning profitability with ethical considerations isn't just a Stoic ideal—it's a strategic imperative. Companies that adopt this Stoic perspective, viewing profitability and ethics as complementary rather than contradictory, position themselves for long-term success, trust, and a legacy that transcends mere balance sheets.

Decision-making in Complex Scenarios

The business world is fraught with complexity. Leaders frequently encounter situations where the right course of action isn't clear-cut, where competing interests, values, and potential outcomes converge. In these gray areas, the Stoic philosophy offers valuable guidance, emphasising rationality, reflection, and moral integrity.

Marcus Aurelius once remarked, *"The best revenge is not to be like your enemy."* In the turbulent world of business, where competition can be fierce, and unethical tactics might seem alluring, this Stoic wisdom reminds leaders to maintain their integrity. Instead of succumbing to questionable practices, Stoicism teaches us to rise above and maintain our ethical standards, even when faced with challenging decisions.

Another Stoic philosopher, Hierocles, provides insight into the interconnectedness of human endeavours, stating, *"We should feel toward the whole human race as we feel toward our fellow citizens."* This Stoic sentiment can guide businesses in their global operations, ensuring respect, fairness, and understanding are at the forefront, regardless of geographical or cultural boundaries.

Case Studies (Fictional)

Case Study 1: Navigating International Expansion

Background
"GlobalTech," a leading multinational corporation in the technology sector, aimed to expand its operations into "EmeraldLand," a developing country known for its vast market potential. However, as GlobalTech ventured into this new territory, they were confronted with a common local practice: the expectation of monetary incentives or "facilitation payments" to expedite permits, licenses, and other essential bureaucratic processes.

The Dilemma
While such payments were customary in EmeraldLand, they posed ethical concerns for GlobalTech. The company prided itself on its transparent operations and had a strict code of conduct against bribery and corruption. Succumbing to local pressures could provide short-term gains but risked long-term reputation damage, potential legal repercussions, and a deviation from the company's core values.

Stoic Intervention
Inspired by the Stoic teachings, GlobalTech's leadership revisited the words of Epictetus: *"What upsets people is not things themselves but their judgments about these things."* Instead of viewing the situation as a roadblock, they saw an opportunity. They realised that while they couldn't control external expectations, they could control their actions and responses.

The Decision
Rejecting the path of facilitation payments, GlobalTech decided to invest in community development projects in EmeraldLand. They collaborated with local NGOs (Non-Governmental Organisations) to build schools, healthcare

clinics, and infrastructure. This not only generated goodwill among the local population but also showcased GlobalTech's commitment to sustainable and responsible business practices.

Outcome
Local authorities, seeing the tangible benefits brought by GlobalTech to their communities, became more supportive of the company's endeavours. The bureaucracy, which initially seemed insurmountable, was streamlined. GlobalTech not only established its operations successfully but also set a precedent for other international corporations entering EmeraldLand.

Through this approach, GlobalTech exemplified the Stoic principle of turning obstacles into opportunities. By focusing on long-term benefits and ethical practices, they achieved sustainable expansion, reinforcing the idea that virtue and success can, and should, go hand in hand.

Case Study 2: Addressing Product Failures

Background
"HealthVita," a well-respected pharmaceutical company, had recently launched "PureLife," a drug intended to combat chronic respiratory diseases. Within months of its release, reports began to surface regarding unexpected side effects in a small percentage of patients, leading to significant health concerns.

The Dilemma
The stakes were high. On one hand, pulling "PureLife" from the market would result in significant financial losses, tarnish the company's reputation, and potentially jeopardise its stock value. On the other, continuing its sales without addressing the concerns risked compromising patient safety and the company's integrity.

Stoic Intervention

The leadership team of HealthVita, familiar with Stoic philosophy, turned to Marcus Aurelius' words for guidance: *"Never esteem anything as of advantage to you that will make you break your word or lose your self-respect."* The Stoic teachings reminded them that external factors, like financial losses, are transient, but one's character and integrity are eternal.

The Decision

Prioritising patient safety and corporate responsibility, HealthVita took the bold step of voluntarily recalling all batches of "PureLife" from the market. They launched an immediate and transparent investigation into the reported side effects, collaborating with external medical experts and researchers. To address the concerns of affected patients, they set up dedicated helplines, provided medical consultations, and offered compensations.

Outcome

While the immediate aftermath saw a dip in HealthVita's stock value and financial performance, the company's forthright approach and commitment to ethical responsibility earned them accolades from industry experts, healthcare professionals, and the general public. In time, with the root cause identified and addressed, a revised version of "PureLife" was introduced to the market, regaining trust and surpassing its initial sales projections.

HealthVita's handling of the crisis not only salvaged their reputation but also reinforced their commitment to ethical business practices, setting a benchmark for the industry.

Through Stoic philosophy, businesses can find a compass to guide them in the murkiest of waters. By focusing on virtue, rationality, and the broader good, leaders can navigate complex scenarios with confidence, ensuring decisions that stand the test of time and scrutiny.

Stakeholders and the Common Good

In the vast landscape of business decisions, the ripple effects of every choice often go beyond the immediate stakeholders to affect the larger community. Stoicism, grounded in understanding humanity's interconnectedness, offers profound insights into this sphere.

Seneca once said, *"We are all bound together in a partnership, and no one man can be independent of others. For we have a common interest, and nature, the mother of us all, has endowed us with mutual affection, making us prone to friendships."* This Stoic view underscores the idea that businesses are not isolated entities; they are part of a broader ecosystem. Every decision they make, intentional or not, impacts this ecosystem.

Historically, businesses have sometimes been myopic, focusing on short-term gains, often to the detriment of the broader society. However, the Stoic belief in the importance of the common good serves as a reminder that long-term success lies in harmonising one's actions with the welfare of all. In a business context, this emphasises that decisions which do not benefit the larger ecosystem will eventually not be beneficial for the business itself.

To align business decisions with broader societal benefits, here are a few Stoic-inspired strategies:

Strategy 1: Stakeholder Inclusion

In the intricate web of modern business, every decision a company makes has the potential to impact a variety of individuals and entities, both directly and indirectly. From employees to investors, customers to local communities, suppliers to competitors, the reverberations of a single business move can be far-reaching. This brings to the forefront the importance of stakeholder inclusion.

Seneca's insight that *"We are parts of a larger whole"* resonates profoundly in this context. Recognising that businesses are not isolated entities but components of a broader system emphasises the significance of including diverse voices in the decision-making process.

Diverse Perspectives Lead to Robust Decisions: By actively involving a wide range of stakeholders, businesses can gather diverse viewpoints, concerns, and insights. This diversity in thought can lead to a more comprehensive understanding of potential challenges and opportunities, allowing for decisions that are well-rounded and thoroughly considered.

Building Trust and Transparency: Engaging stakeholders in the decision-making process fosters transparency. When stakeholders feel their voices are heard and considered, it nurtures trust. This trust is foundational for building long-lasting relationships, be it with customers, employees, or investors.

Anticipating and Mitigating Challenges: Including diverse stakeholders can also help businesses anticipate challenges. For instance, by involving local communities in decisions related to infrastructure projects, businesses can foresee potential socio-environmental challenges and address them proactively.

Ensuring Ethical Decisions: Stakeholder inclusion is also a means to ensure that business decisions are ethically sound. By considering the interests and concerns of all affected parties, businesses are more likely to make decisions that align with broader societal values and the common good.

Driving Innovation and Opportunities: Diverse stakeholder perspectives can also be a source of innovation. Different viewpoints can bring forth novel ideas, solutions, and opportunities that might not have been evident from a narrower viewpoint.

In essence, stakeholder inclusion is not just a Stoic-inspired ethical imperative but also a strategic one. By embracing the collective wisdom of diverse groups, businesses can make decisions that are not only ethically sound but also strategically robust, ensuring sustainable success in the long run.

Strategy 2: Long-term Visioning: A Sustainable Approach to Business

In today's fast-paced business landscape, it's easy to get caught up in the race for immediate profits and short-term gains. However, a narrow focus on immediate results can often jeopardise the long-term sustainability and success of a business. Herein lies the importance of long-term visioning, an approach that prioritises future sustainability and value creation over short-term profitability.

Marcus Aurelius once said, *"Think of the whole universe as one living being, having one substance and one soul; and observe how all things have reference to one perception, the perception of this one living being."* This Stoic perspective underscores the interconnectedness of all things and emphasises the importance of considering the broader, long-term picture.

Beyond Immediate Profits: While immediate profits are essential for operational viability, a hyper-focus on them can lead to decisions that might harm the business in the long run. For instance, cutting corners in product quality might boost profits now but could damage the brand's reputation over time.

Sustainability and Ethical Considerations: Long-term visioning ensures that businesses adopt sustainable practices, both environmentally and socially. By prioritising sustainability, businesses not only protect the environment but also ensure their operations remain viable in a world increasingly affected by climate change and societal demands for ethical practices.

Building Lasting Relationships: A long-term vision fosters stronger relationships with stakeholders. Whether it's customers, suppliers, employees, or investors, showing a commitment to long-term value creation fosters trust and loyalty, vital components for sustainable business success.

Future-proofing the Business: By focusing on long-term strategies, businesses are better prepared to adapt to future challenges and disruptions. Whether it's technological advancements, changing consumer preferences, or global economic shifts, long-term visioning equips businesses with the flexibility and foresight to navigate these changes.

Value Creation for All: Long-term visioning is about creating value not just for shareholders, but for all stakeholders. This includes employees, customers, local communities, and society at large. By ensuring that the business remains a beneficial force in society, it safeguards its social license to operate, which is becoming increasingly important in today's socially-conscious business environment.

In the words of Seneca, *"As is a tale, so is life: not how long it is, but how good it is, is what matters."* Similarly, in business, it's not just about immediate results, but the lasting legacy and impact a company leaves behind. By adopting a long-term vision, businesses can ensure they remain relevant, respected, and beneficial forces in society for years to come.

Strategy 3: Ethical Auditing: Proactive Reflection for Ethical Business Operations

In the complex and ever-evolving world of business, it is not uncommon for organisations to sometimes lose sight of their ethical compass amidst the myriad challenges and pressures they face. While it is essential to address problems and lapses as they occur, a more proactive approach can often prevent these issues in the first place. Enter the concept of **ethical auditing** – a systematic evaluation of an organisation's adherence to ethical standards and practices.

Drawing inspiration from Epictetus's profound insight, *"It's not what happens to you, but how you react to it that matters,"* ethical auditing is not merely about responding to dilemmas but is rooted in the Stoic principle of introspection and proactive action. Here's a deeper dive into its significance:

Continuous Monitoring: Just as businesses routinely conduct financial audits to ensure fiscal responsibility and compliance, ethical audits provide a regular check on a company's moral and social responsibilities. It's a structured process that examines policies, practices, and outcomes from an ethical perspective.

Identifying Potential Risks: By proactively identifying areas where ethical breaches could occur, businesses can address potential vulnerabilities before they become significant issues. This could range from supply chain practices, employee welfare, environmental concerns, to marketing strategies.

Stakeholder Trust and Reputation: Ethical auditing reinforces an organisation's commitment to its values, boosting trust among stakeholders, including customers, investors, employees, and the broader community. A strong ethical reputation can differentiate a brand in a crowded marketplace and foster long-term loyalty.

Guided Decision-making: Having a clear understanding of ethical standards and potential pitfalls can guide future decision-making processes, ensuring that ethics are at the forefront of strategic choices.

Creating a Culture of Integrity: Regular ethical auditing instills a culture of integrity and moral responsibility throughout the organisation. It empowers employees at all levels to uphold and champion ethical standards in their day-to-day operations.

Continuous Improvement and Adaptation: The world is constantly changing, and what is considered ethical now might evolve in the future. Regular ethical audits ensure that businesses adapt to these changes, updating their practices and policies to reflect contemporary ethical standards.

Protection Against Legal Repercussions: Many ethical breaches can lead to legal consequences. Proactively addressing these through ethical audits can save businesses from costly legal battles and potential regulatory penalties.

In the words of Seneca, "*We should every night call ourselves to an account; What infirmity have I mastered today? What passions opposed? What temptation resisted? What virtue acquired?*" Similarly, businesses must continually reflect on their actions, ensure they align with ethical principles, and proactively work towards a better, more responsible future. Ethical auditing provides the tools and framework to do just that.

In essence, Stoicism's emphasis on the interconnectedness of society and the importance of the common good provides a robust framework for businesses. It pushes them to rise above narrow objectives and strive for a harmony that benefits all, encapsulating the very essence of ethical decision-making.

Navigating Biases and Emotional Triggers

In the intricate tapestry of business decision-making, biases and emotional triggers often lurk beneath the surface, subtly influencing choices and leading us astray from rational judgment. Stoicism, with its emphasis on self-awareness, introspection, and rationality, offers invaluable insights to navigate these challenges and make decisions that align with both ethical standards and business objectives.

As Marcus Aurelius once remarked, *"You have power over your mind – not outside events. Realise this, and you will find strength."* This sentiment underscores the Stoic belief in inner control and the ability to discern between our reactions and external events.

A Stoic Approach to Self-awareness and Introspection:

Recognising and Challenging Biases
Our minds, influenced by past experiences, cultural norms, and personal beliefs, often harbour biases. A Stoic approach emphasises recognising these biases through introspection. As Seneca noted, *"We suffer more often in imagination than in reality."* By challenging these biases, we can see situations more objectively, ensuring that our decisions aren't swayed by unfounded beliefs or assumptions.

Emotional Mastery

Emotions are a natural part of the human experience, but when unchecked, they can cloud judgment. Stoicism teaches us to observe our emotions without being controlled by them. By mastering our emotional responses, we can approach decision-making with clarity and calm, even in high-pressure situations.

Techniques to Ensure Rationality and Avoid Common Pitfalls:

The View from Above Technique

This Stoic practice involves visualising a situation from a broader perspective, much like looking down from a high vantage point. This helps in detaching from immediate emotional reactions and seeing the bigger picture.

Premeditatio Malorum (Negative Visualisation)

By visualising potential negative outcomes, we can better prepare for them and even work to prevent them. This technique also helps in distinguishing between genuine concerns and baseless worries.

Dichotomy of Control

Recognising what's within our control and what isn't can lead to more focused and effective decision-making. By concentrating our efforts on areas we can influence and accepting those we cannot, we can avoid unnecessary stress and remain action-oriented.

Reflective Journaling

A regular practice of journaling can help in introspection and recognising patterns in our decision-making, biases, and triggers. By penning down thoughts, challenges, and reflections, we can achieve greater clarity and self-awareness.

In the complex realm of business, where decisions often have far-reaching consequences, the Stoic emphasis on self-awareness, emotional mastery, and rationality becomes invaluable. By adopting these Stoic techniques and principles, business leaders and teams can navigate the labyrinth of biases and emotional triggers, making decisions that are not only ethically sound but also strategically astute.

Stoic Strategies for Crisis Decisions

In the tumultuous world of business, crises are inevitable. Whether it's a market downturn, an unforeseen disruption, or an internal organisational challenge, leaders are often called upon to make critical decisions under immense pressure. Stoicism, with its emphasis on calmness, rationality, and virtue, provides a solid foundation for navigating these stormy waters. As the Stoic philosopher Seneca aptly stated, *"Fire tests gold, suffering tests brave men."*

Guiding Principles for Decision-making during Times of Organisational or Market Crises:

Maintaining Composure
In the face of adversity, a Stoic remains calm, understanding that emotional reactions can cloud judgment. As Marcus Aurelius reminds us, *"If you are distressed by anything external, the pain is not due to the thing itself, but to your estimate of it; and this you have the power to revoke at any moment."* By maintaining emotional equilibrium, leaders can better assess the situation and make informed decisions.

Focus on What's Controllable
Crises often bring a sense of chaos and unpredictability. However, Stoicism teaches us the importance of focusing on what is within our control. This empowers leaders to take actionable steps rather than getting overwhelmed by external circumstances.

Ethical Integrity

Even in challenging times, Stoicism emphasises the importance of maintaining ethical integrity. As Seneca said, *"A gem cannot be polished without friction, nor a man perfected without trials."* Leaders should strive to make decisions that align with core values and principles, regardless of external pressures.

Long-term Vision

While immediate challenges demand attention, Stoic leaders also consider the long-term implications of their decisions, ensuring that short-term solutions don't compromise future stability and growth.

Examples (Fictional) of Stoic Leadership During Challenging Times

The Airline CEO

In the late 2000s, the aviation industry faced one of its most significant challenges. Economic downturns, fluctuating fuel prices, and global uncertainties led many airlines to the brink of bankruptcy. Amidst this backdrop, the story of one particular airline CEO stands out as a testament to Stoic leadership.

David, the CEO of AeroFly Airlines, found his company grappling with plummeting revenues and rising operational costs. Analysts predicted massive layoffs, and employees braced for the worst. But David, having been influenced by Stoic philosophy, approached the situation differently.

1. **Personal Sacrifice for the Greater Good:** Before considering any staff reductions, David announced a voluntary 50% cut to his salary. He was joined by his executive team, who followed suit with significant pay reductions. This move was rooted in the Stoic principle of

fairness and the belief, as Epictetus once said, *"What is the goal of virtue, after all, except a life that flows smoothly?"*

2. **Transparent Communication:** Instead of keeping employees in the dark, David held town hall meetings, openly discussing the company's financial challenges and seeking input on cost-saving measures. This decision underscored the Stoic value of treating all individuals with respect and dignity, recognising the inherent wisdom of the collective.

3. **Innovative Solutions over Layoffs:** Rather than resorting to immediate layoffs, the company introduced voluntary unpaid leave, flexible working hours, and job-sharing initiatives. Many employees opted for these, valuing job security over short-term income loss. This approach not only preserved jobs but also maintained company morale, a decision reflecting the Stoic emphasis on the interconnectedness of society and the importance of the common good.

4. **Stoic Resilience:** Despite the challenging times, David regularly quoted Marcus Aurelius's wisdom: *"Out of difficulties grow miracles."* He encouraged his team to view the crisis as an opportunity to innovate, streamline, and emerge stronger.

Under David's Stoic leadership, AeroFly Airlines not only weathered the storm but also emerged as an industry leader in employee satisfaction and operational efficiency. The decisions made during the crisis cemented AeroFly's reputation as a company that genuinely valued its employees and operated with integrity, even in the face of adversity.

In reflecting on the challenging period, David often emphasised the Stoic belief in the power of virtuous action, echoing Seneca's words: *"It is the power of the mind to be unconquerable.* " Through his actions, David showcased how Stoic principles, when applied in leadership, can transform challenges into opportunities for growth and renewed strength.

The Green Energy Pioneer

In the early 2010s, the green energy sector was still in its nascent stages, grappling with technological challenges, wavering government support, and stiff competition from established fossil fuel industries. Amid this tumultuous backdrop, the story of Lina, the founder and CEO of SolTech Energies, stands out as a masterclass in Stoic leadership.

Lina's dream was to revolutionise the energy market with sustainable solutions, and she launched SolTech with this vision. However, the journey was anything but smooth.

1. **Unwavering Commitment to Vision:** Despite facing skepticism from industry veterans and investors alike, Lina remained steadfast in her belief in green energy's potential. Drawing inspiration from the Stoic philosopher Epictetus, who said, *"First say to yourself what you would be; and then do what you have to do."* Lina continuously invested in research and development, even when short-term gains were uncertain.

2. **Embracing Setbacks as Opportunities:** When a prototype of a new solar panel failed during a public demonstration, instead of panicking or deflecting blame, Lina addressed the situation head-on. She openly acknowledged the failure and used it as a learning opportunity. This approach mirrored the Stoic belief, as articulated by Marcus Aurelius: *"The impediment to action advances action. What stands in the way becomes the way."* Under Lina's guidance, the team revisited the design, leading to a breakthrough innovation in solar energy capture.

3. **Prioritising Ethical Business Practices:** Lina was often faced with choices that could provide quick profits but compromise on ethical standards, be it sourcing materials or labour practices. Guided by the Stoic principle of justice and integrity, she consistently chose the ethical path, even if it meant higher costs or longer timelines. Her commitment to doing right resonated with Seneca's words: *"A good character, when it is once settled in a resolution, does not call itself back. It is not led astray by any idle reflections."*

4. Leading with Empathy and Collaboration: Understanding that the green energy revolution was bigger than any single company, Lina often collaborated with competitors, sharing research findings and co-funding projects. This collective approach, rooted in the Stoic understanding of mutual interdependence, accelerated the sector's growth and cemented SolTech's position as a pioneer.

Under Lina's leadership, SolTech Energies not only thrived financially but also played a pivotal role in transforming the public's perception of green energy. Lina's Stoic approach to leadership—emphasising vision, resilience, ethics, and collaboration—proved that businesses could be both profitable and principled, even in the face of significant challenges.

The Tech Visionary
In the fiercely competitive world of technology startups, the story of Julian, the founder of CyberTech Innovations, stands as a testament to the power of Stoic leadership. Julian's journey from a basement coder to the head of a global tech empire wasn't without its hurdles, but his Stoic approach helped him navigate the tumultuous tech waters with grace and determination.

1. **Embracing Uncertainty with Grace:** At the dawn of the internet era, Julian envisioned a world interconnected through groundbreaking software solutions. However, with rapid technological changes and unpredictable market trends, the tech landscape was riddled with uncertainty. Drawing inspiration from Seneca's words, *"We suffer more often in imagination than in reality,"* Julian learned to differentiate between genuine threats and mere perceived risks. This perspective allowed him to take calculated risks and seize opportunities that others often overlooked.

2. **Adapting and Evolving:** When CyberTech's first product faced obsolescence due to an unexpected industry shift, Julian didn't wallow in despair. Instead, echoing Marcus Aurelius's sentiment, *"The universe is change; our life is what our thoughts make it"* he rallied his team to pivot and adapt. This adaptability became CyberTech's hallmark, ensuring its survival and growth in a volatile market.

3. **Building Relationships over Transactions:** In an industry often criticised for prioritising profits over people, Julian stood out. He believed in cultivating deep relationships with both clients and employees. Taking to heart Epictetus's teaching, *"Wealth consists not in having great possessions, but in having few wants"* Julian focused on creating value rather than mere profit. This approach fostered loyalty, turned clients into long-term partners, and made CyberTech a sought-after employer.

4. **Valuing Feedback and Self-Reflection:** Julian was never one to rest on his laurels. He created a culture at CyberTech where feedback, even if critical, was valued. By inviting diverse opinions and being open to self-reflection, Julian ensured CyberTech's continuous growth and innovation.

Under Julian's Stoic leadership, CyberTech Innovations not only became a tech powerhouse but also a beacon of ethical and sustainable business practices in the tech world. His journey demonstrated that with a Stoic approach, leaders could not only navigate challenges but turn them into stepping stones for greater achievements.

Stoicism offers timeless wisdom for leaders navigating the complexities of crisis decision-making. By grounding decisions in Stoic virtues and principles, leaders can not only navigate challenges with grace and integrity but also pave the way for long-term success and resilience.

Integrating Stoicism into Organisational Decision-making Processes

In today's fast-paced and complex business environment, decision-making is both an art and a science. As organisations grapple with a myriad of choices every day, the wisdom of Stoicism aids clarity, ensuring that these decisions are both informed and ethical. But how can modern businesses integrate this ancient philosophy into their everyday decision-making processes?

Begin with a Stoic Audit
Before embarking on the journey of integrating Stoicism, organisations must understand their current decision-making landscape. Conducting a Stoic audit involves examining past decisions, identifying areas of improvement, and understanding the current organisational ethos. This introspective step lays the foundation for a meaningful Stoic transformation.

Organisational Training and Workshops
Once the groundwork is laid, businesses should invest in training programs that introduce employees to Stoic principles. Workshops focused on Stoic virtues, the Dichotomy of Control, and Stoic reflections can be immensely beneficial. In the words of Seneca, *"As long as you live, keep*

learning how to live. " Continuous learning and reflection on Stoic teachings can transform the decision-making fabric of an organisation.

Stoic Decision-making Frameworks
Introduce decision-making frameworks that incorporate Stoic principles. For instance, before making a significant decision, teams can be encouraged to evaluate options based on Stoic virtues like wisdom, courage, justice, and temperance. As Marcus Aurelius advised, *"Look beneath the surface; let not the several quality of a thing nor its worth escape thee."* By delving deep and considering the broader implications, businesses can make choices that stand the test of time.

Leadership Programs
The top echelons of management play a crucial role in setting the tone for decision-making. Specialised leadership programs can be introduced, focusing on Stoic leadership, ensuring that the leaders are equipped to guide their teams with Stoic wisdom. Leaders can draw inspiration from the Stoic emphasis on leading by example, ensuring that decisions at the highest levels resonate with Stoic values.

Feedback and Continuous Improvement
Embrace the Stoic spirit of self-improvement by actively seeking feedback on decision-making processes. Encourage a culture where employees, stakeholders, and even customers can provide insights into how decisions impact them. This feedback loop, rooted in Stoic teachings, ensures that the organisation remains adaptable and responsive.

Integrating Stoicism into organisational decision-making processes is not just about adopting a set of principles; it's about embracing a mindset shift. By taking practical steps and fostering an environment of continuous learning and reflection, businesses can ensure that their decisions are not just profitable but also ethical, sustainable, and aligned with the greater good.

Conclusion

The journey through this chapter has taken us into the heart of Stoic philosophy, illuminating its profound relevance to the challenges and opportunities faced by modern businesses. As we have discovered, Stoic principles don't merely offer abstract wisdom; they provide actionable insights, shaping the way businesses approach decisions, ensuring they are rooted in ethics, long-term vision, and a commitment to the greater good.

To reiterate the profound words of Seneca, *"We are more often frightened than hurt; and we suffer more in imagination than in reality."* In the context of business, this teaches us to differentiate between perceived and real challenges, guiding us to approach problems with clarity and rationality. By adopting Stoic wisdom, businesses can navigate the tumultuous seas of uncertainty with an unwavering compass.

The value of Stoicism in decision-making isn't just about being rational or ethical; it's about aligning one's business practices with virtues that stand the test of time. As Musonius Rufus said, *"That which is truly good and beneficial for humans is always achievable, and that which is achievable is not difficult."* This Stoic sentiment encourages businesses to strive for what is truly beneficial, ensuring success that is both meaningful and sustainable.

It's essential to understand that the wisdom offered by Stoicism isn't merely a tool or strategy; it's a mindset. A transformative mindset that, once internalised, can catalyse remarkable growth, innovation, and sustainable success in any business venture. As we venture deeper into the chapters ahead, let the teachings of Stoicism be a guiding light, illuminating the path to both professional and personal excellence.

In closing, a final reflection from Marcus Aurelius serves as a powerful call to action: *"The best revenge is to be unlike him who performed the injury."* In the world of business, where competition and rivalry are often fierce, let Stoicism inspire us to rise above petty conflicts, focusing instead on creating value, building trust, and ensuring a legacy that future generations can be proud of.

As we set our sights on the chapters to come, may the Stoic journey inspire, challenge, and transform every reader's approach to business, leadership, and life itself.

Step 5
Realising Stoic Principles in
Business Operations

Chapter 9
Transforming Theory into Practice: Stoicism in Daily Operations

In our journey through "Stoicism at the Summit," we've ventured deep into the heart of Stoic philosophy, uncovering its principles, virtues, and the transformative potential it holds for modern businesses. From leadership approaches to decision-making frameworks, we've seen how Stoic teachings can elevate every facet of an organisation. As Seneca once noted, *"It's not because things are difficult that we dare not venture. It's because we dare not venture that they are difficult."* This wisdom reminds us that the challenges in applying Stoic principles in daily operations are not insurmountable; they simply require a daring spirit.

While the earlier chapters provided a theoretical foundation, the real test lies in the application. It's one thing to understand Stoicism and quite another to weave it into the fabric of a business's daily operations. As Marcus Aurelius aptly put it, *"Waste no more time arguing what a good man should be. Be one."* This sentiment is the crux of our current exploration. It's about being the embodiment of Stoic virtues every day, in every business decision and operation.

However, the challenge is evident. The bustling world of business, with its pressing deadlines, evolving challenges, and diverse stakeholders, often pushes organisations towards short-termism. Amidst this, how does one stay true to the Stoic emphasis on long-term vision, ethical grounding, and the greater common good? How do businesses ensure that the Stoic principles are not just reserved for leadership decisions but are also reflected in the day-to-day tasks, processes, and interactions?

This chapter is dedicated to addressing these very questions. We'll look at practical strategies, applications, and case studies that showcase businesses transforming Stoic theory into daily practice, setting the gold standard for operational excellence. As Epictetus wisely said, *"First learn the meaning of what you say, and then speak."* And so, before we speak of Stoic practices, let's ensure we deeply understand its meaning and how it translates into the daily grind of business operations.

The Stoic Operational Framework

Echoing the wisdom of the Stoic teacher Chrysippus, who understood destiny as *'a series of causes chained together'*, this speaks to the need for distinct strategic intentions - a master plan - that transforms every unexpected event into an opportunity for advancement. Like a climber uses the terrain to ascend the summit, businesses armed with a Stoic framework can skilfully ascend the competitive peaks of the industry with poise and resilience.

Blueprint for Stoic Assimilation

Central to the Stoic operational framework is a deliberate strategy that integrates Stoic ethics into all aspects of company practice. This is initiated by:

Charting a Stoic Course
Defining a future for the organisation that is deeply rooted in Stoic ethics. Echoing the insight of Socrates, who believed in the power of a clear self-definition, *'An unexamined life is not worth living.'* This course serves as a beacon, steering all business tactics and activities.

Moral Base
Committing to ethical practices across all business operations, from supply chain to client interactions, is crucial. This reflects the Stoic principle of acting virtuously, aiming for the well-being of not just the business but the broader community. *'We are not born for ourselves alone,'* highlights the notion that business practices should have a positive impact on all involved parties.

Persistent Self-Examination and Enhancement
Embracing Stoic thought entails an ongoing introspection and pursuit of excellence. Through consistent evaluation and refinement of business practices according to Stoic ideals, firms can maintain their commitment to a course of ethical and sustainable progression.

Adapting Stoicism Across the Business Spectrum

Stoicism, with its universal principles, is versatile. Whether it's a tech startup in Silicon Valley, a manufacturing unit in the industrial heartlands, or a global retail chain, the core tenets of Stoicism remain relevant.

Emphasise the Stoic values of **integrity and fairness** in all customer interactions. In service sectors for example, it's crucial to address customers' concerns proactively, ensuring their imagined fears are alleviated by the reality of impeccable service.

Focus on the Stoic principles of **simplicity and efficiency**. Ensure that resources are utilised optimally, waste is minimised, and the well-being of workers is prioritised.

Lean into the Stoic virtues of **wisdom and courage**. While the rapidly changing business landscape can be daunting, a

Stoic approach encourages businesses to embrace change, innovate ethically, and always keep the greater good in mind.

In essence, the Stoic operational framework is not a rigid set of rules but a flexible guide, adaptable and relevant to every business model. By grounding operations in Stoic principles, businesses not only ensure ethical and sustainable practices but also position themselves for long-term success in an ever-evolving corporate landscape.

Operational Efficiency Through Stoic Simplicity

In the context of business operations Stoicism highlights the value of simplicity — not just for the sake of minimalism, but as a means to achieve greater efficiency and clarity in the business process.

The Stoic Value of Simplicity in Business

A business operation laden with complexities and redundancies is akin to a ship weighed down by excess cargo; it moves slowly and is prone to falter. Stoicism teaches us the importance of discerning the essential from the non-essential, ensuring that every action, every process, directly contributes to the larger objective.

As the Stoic philosopher Seneca noted, *"It's not the man who has too little but the man who craves more, that is poor."* This quote encapsulates the idea that businesses should focus on the essentials, ensuring that every operational aspect serves a clear purpose. By doing so, they can avoid the pitfalls of overextension and inefficiency.

Steps to Achieve Stoic Simplicity in Operations

Audit and Assess
Begin by undertaking a comprehensive audit of all operational processes. Identify redundancies, bottlenecks, and areas where complexity has added no tangible value. Remember the words of Marcus Aurelius, *"Ask yourself at every moment, 'Is this necessary?'"* This reflective approach ensures that only essential processes remain.

Streamline and Standardise
After identifying areas of improvement, work towards streamlining processes. This might involve adopting new technologies, retraining staff, or reorganising departments. The goal is to ensure that every operation is as efficient and straightforward as possible.

Foster a Culture of Simplicity
Encourage employees at all levels to embrace the Stoic value of simplicity. By fostering a culture where employees are empowered to question unnecessary complexities and champion streamlined processes, businesses can ensure that the principle of Stoic simplicity is embedded in their operational DNA.

Regularly Review and Refine
Simplicity is not a one-time achievement but an ongoing pursuit. Regularly review operations to ensure that they remain streamlined and free from unnecessary complexities. This iterative approach ensures that the business remains agile and adaptable.

By embracing the Stoic principle of simplicity, businesses can achieve operational efficiency, ensuring that they are well-positioned to navigate the challenges of the modern corporate landscape. Through regular reflection, streamlining, and an emphasis on the essential, companies can drive growth while staying true to Stoic values.

Stoic Mindset in Employee Onboarding and Training

"The key is to keep company only with people who uplift you, whose presence calls forth your best," wrote Epictetus. His words resonate deeply when considering the onboarding and training of new employees. Ensuring that new members assimilate the values and principles of the company is pivotal, and integrating Stoic philosophy can be a transformative approach to ensuring a harmonious and productive workplace.

Stoic Values in Onboarding

Introduction to Stoicism
Begin the onboarding process with an introduction to the core Stoic principles. This can be a workshop or an interactive session where new hires are familiarised with Stoic concepts such as the Dichotomy of Control, the four virtues (wisdom, courage, justice, temperance), and the Stoic focus on character and integrity.

Alignment with Company Values
Draw parallels between Stoic virtues and the company's core values. Show new hires how these values are not just theoretical concepts but are lived and breathed in every business operation.

Scenario-based Learning
Use real-world scenarios where Stoic principles can be applied. Teach new employees to perceive challenges as opportunities for growth, echoing this Stoic sentiment.

Continuous Stoic-Based Learning and Development

Ongoing Workshops
Organise regular workshops where Stoic principles are discussed in the context of daily business challenges. Utilise quotes and teachings from Stoic philosophers like Marcus Aurelius, who noted, *"Our life is what our thoughts make it."* Emphasise the importance of a positive, proactive mindset in navigating business challenges.

Feedback and Reflection
Encourage employees to adopt the Stoic practice of daily reflection. Create feedback mechanisms where employees can reflect on their actions, decisions, and their alignment with Stoic virtues.

Scenario-based Training Modules
Incorporate Stoic teachings into training modules. For instance, when training sales teams, emphasise the Stoic principle of integrity and honesty in all dealings.

Mentorship Programs
Establish mentorship programs where seasoned employees, well-versed in the company's Stoic values, guide and train newer members. This not only ensures the transmission of Stoic principles but also fosters a culture of mutual respect and growth.

Integrating Stoicism into the onboarding and continuous training processes ensures that employees are not just skilled in their respective roles but are also aligned with the company's core values. It guarantees that the workforce is equipped not just to perform their tasks but to do so with wisdom, integrity, and a genuine commitment to the common good. The Stoic mindset, when incorporated into training, lays the foundation for operational excellence and a harmonious, productive work environment.

Stoic Conflict Resolution in Operations

Conflict is an inevitable part of business operations. Whether it's disagreements over project directions, clashes between team members, or disputes with external stakeholders, businesses are no strangers to conflict. However, how these conflicts are approached and resolved can significantly impact an organisation's success and culture. Stoicism offers a unique, calm, and rational approach to conflict resolution, emphasising understanding, virtue, and the common good.

Techniques Grounded in Stoic Wisdom

Understanding the Dichotomy of Control
Recognising what is within our control and what isn't is a fundamental Stoic principle. In conflict situations, this means focusing on our reactions, decisions, and actions, rather than attempting to control external factors or other individuals' choices. As Epictetus advised, *"In life, our first job is this, to divide and distinguish things into two categories: externals I cannot control, but the choices I make with regard to them I do control."*

Seeking Mutual Understanding
Marcus Aurelius once said, *"Whenever you are about to find fault with someone, ask yourself the following question: What fault of mine most nearly resembles the one I am about to criticise?"* This emphasises the importance of empathy and understanding in conflict situations. Before jumping to conclusions, strive to understand the other party's perspective.

Prioritising the Common Good
A Stoic is always focused on the broader picture, emphasising the benefit of the collective over individual gain. In conflicts, this means looking for solutions that are mutually beneficial and promote the common good.

Emphasising Virtues over Ego
Conflicts often escalate when parties let their egos take the front seat. Stoicism teaches the value of virtues like wisdom, courage, justice, and temperance. In conflict resolution, this translates to making decisions that are fair, just, and grounded in reason rather than personal ego.

Case Studies (Fictional)

Case Study 1: Project Direction Disagreements

In a rapidly evolving tech landscape, a leading software development company, ZenTech, was embarking on a groundbreaking project that had the potential to revolutionise the industry. The project was a new platform aimed at simplifying cloud storage solutions for both businesses and individual users. However, as development progressed, a significant disagreement arose between two senior developers, Alex and Priya.

The Core of the Disagreement
Alex, with a decade of experience in software architecture, believed that the platform should be built using a microservices architecture. He argued that this would make the platform more scalable and easier to maintain. His vision was a system that could efficiently handle large volumes of data transactions without any performance hitches.

Priya, on the other hand, had a background in user experience and front-end development. She believed that while scalability was essential, the primary focus should be on user experience and interface design. She felt that a monolithic architecture, which is simpler but can be less scalable, would allow for a more cohesive and user-friendly design.

The Stoic-Guided Resolution

Rather than letting the disagreement stall the project, the project manager, an advocate of Stoic principles, intervened. Recognising the value both perspectives brought, he initiated a series of Stoic-guided discussions.

1. **Understanding and Empathy:** Using Marcus Aurelius's wisdom, *"Look beneath the surface; let not the several quality of a thing nor its worth escape thee,"* the project manager encouraged Alex and Priya to delve deep into each other's viewpoints. They spent time shadowing each other, with Alex understanding the intricacies of user design and Priya grasping the scalability concerns.

2. **Dichotomy of Control:** The project manager reminded them of Epictetus's teaching about focusing on what's within one's control. Instead of dwelling on their differences, they were encouraged to find areas of collaboration and synergy.

3. **Common Good:** Keeping the broader project goal in mind, they were reminded of the Stoic emphasis on the collective's benefit. Both developers agreed that the project's success was paramount, and personal egos should not hinder it.

The Outcome

After several discussions and collaborative sessions, a hybrid solution was proposed. The platform would be built using a microservices architecture, as Alex suggested, ensuring scalability and performance. However, a dedicated team, led by Priya, would focus exclusively on user interface and experience, ensuring that the platform was not only robust but also user-friendly.

The project was a resounding success, with ZenTech receiving accolades for its innovative approach. Both Alex and Priya, having learned the value of understanding and collaboration, went on to lead other successful projects in the company, always keeping Stoic principles at the heart of their decision-making.

Case Study 2: Vendor-Client Disputes

ClearWater Solutions, a global water purification equipment manufacturer, had landed a massive contract with AquaLife, a chain of high-end health resorts. AquaLife was initiating a new project to provide state-of-the-art spa facilities across its resorts, and ClearWater's equipment was crucial for ensuring the purity and quality of water in these spas.

However, a few months into the installation phase, disagreements arose. AquaLife claimed that some of the equipment delivered by ClearWater did not match the specifications agreed upon in the contract. ClearWater, on the other hand, argued that they had adhered to all stipulated specifications and that any deviations were within accepted industrial standards.

The Core of the Dispute
AquaLife's project managers believed that the equipment's slight deviations could compromise the guest experience. They were aiming for perfection in every aspect of the spa experience, and even minor issues with water quality could tarnish their brand's reputation. ClearWater, having invested significant resources in customising equipment for AquaLife, felt that the deviations were minor and would not impact the water quality. They believed AquaLife was being unnecessarily stringent.

The Stoic-Guided Resolution
Recognising the potential long-term business relationship at stake, both parties agreed to bring in a mediator familiar with Stoic principles to resolve the matter.

1. **Seeking Understanding:** Drawing from Seneca's wisdom, *"We are more often frightened than hurt; and we suffer more from imagination than from reality,"* the mediator set up a demonstration. ClearWater was asked to set up the equipment, and AquaLife's experts assessed the water quality. This practical demonstration clarified that while there were deviations, the water quality was not compromised.

2. **Value of Relationships:** Reminded of Marcus Aurelius's reflection, *"What injures the hive, injures the bee,"* both parties recognised that a damaged business relationship would hurt both companies. They had mutual interests in the project's success.

3. **Compromise and Collaboration:** With Epictetus's advice, *"When you are offended at any man's fault, turn to yourself and study your own failings,"* both parties acknowledged their communication gaps leading up to the dispute. ClearWater accepted that they could have been more transparent about the equipment's capabilities, while AquaLife recognised that they could have provided clearer specifications.

The Outcome

A compromise was reached. ClearWater agreed to replace specific critical equipment components to ensure complete alignment with AquaLife's requirements. In return, AquaLife provided additional time for the installation phase to accommodate these changes. The project was successfully completed, and both companies benefited significantly from their collaboration.

The dispute resolution, guided by Stoic principles, not only salvaged a potentially damaging situation but also strengthened the bond between ClearWater and AquaLife, leading to further collaborations in the future.

Case Study 3: Team Dynamic Challenges

FutureTech, a cutting-edge software development company, had always prided itself on its innovation-driven teams. Comprising talented individuals from diverse backgrounds, the teams were structured to foster creativity and out-of-the-box thinking. However, with diversity came differences in opinions, work styles, and communication patterns. Over time, these differences began to manifest as conflicts, affecting project timelines and overall team morale.

The Core of the Dispute
The design team, passionate about creating user-centric interfaces, often found themselves at odds with the development team, who emphasised the technical feasibility and optimisation of the software. Meetings became battlegrounds, with members becoming increasingly entrenched in their viewpoints. The project's progress stagnated as teams became more focused on internal disputes than on the actual objectives.

The Stoic-Guided Resolution
The company's leadership, recognising the urgency of the situation, decided to engage a Stoic philosophy-trained organisational consultant to address the challenges.

1. **Empathy and Understanding:** Reflecting on Seneca's words, *"One of the most beautiful qualities of true friendship is to understand and to be understood,"* the consultant initiated a series of team-building exercises. These exercises were designed to allow team members to step into each other's shoes, understanding the challenges and constraints each faced.

2. **Shared Objectives:** Drawing inspiration from Marcus Aurelius's insight, *"We are made for cooperation, like feet, like hands, like eyelids, like the rows of the upper and*

lower teeth," the teams were reminded of their shared goal: creating an exceptional product. They were encouraged to view their roles not as individual contributors but as interconnected parts of a larger whole.

3. **Open Communication:** Open forums were established. Here, team members could voice their concerns and challenges without fear of retribution. This fostered a culture of open dialogue, allowing conflicts to be addressed at their nascent stages.

The Outcome

The teams began collaborating more effectively. The design team became more receptive to understanding the technical constraints, and the development team became more attuned to the importance of user experience. This synergy accelerated the project's progress, and the end product was both technically robust and user-friendly.

By addressing team dynamic challenges through the lens of Stoic philosophy, FutureTech not only resolved immediate conflicts but also set the foundation for a more collaborative and understanding work environment in the future.

In summary, Stoicism, with its emphasis on reason, virtue, and the common good, provides a robust framework for conflict resolution in business operations. By adopting a Stoic approach, businesses can navigate conflicts with wisdom, ensuring that decisions made are not just beneficial in the short term but also pave the way for long-term success and harmony.

Supply Chain Management with Stoic Ethics

The supply chain, often seen as the backbone of any business operation, encompasses a vast network of interdependent activities – from sourcing raw materials to the delivery of final products to consumers. While efficiency and cost-effectiveness have long been primary considerations, there's an emerging emphasis on integrating ethics into supply chain management. This is where Stoic philosophy can offer invaluable insights.

Stoic Ethics in Sourcing
Drawing upon Seneca's statement, *"A benefit should be conferred willingly, without reluctance or regret,"* businesses should ensure that the raw materials and products they source are procured under fair conditions. This means avoiding suppliers who exploit their workers, harm the environment, or engage in corrupt practices. The goal is not just to receive, but to ensure that the act of receiving itself is rooted in ethical grounds, bringing mutual benefit to all parties involved.

Stoic Partnerships in Distribution
Marcus Aurelius reminds us, *"We are constituted so as to associate, to feel affection, to help one another."* In the context of supply chain partnerships, this translates to forming alliances with distributors who share the same Stoic values. Collaborating with ethical distributors ensures that products are delivered efficiently without compromising on values, such as ensuring the welfare of logistics staff or minimising environmental impact.

Stoic Values in Supplier Partnerships
Engaging with suppliers is not just a transactional relationship; it's a partnership. Reflecting on Epictetus's wisdom, *"It is not events that disturb people, it is their*

judgments concerning them, " businesses should establish clear communication channels with suppliers. This ensures that any challenges or disagreements are viewed as opportunities for growth and collaboration, rather than adversarial conflicts.

Benefits of Stoic-aligned Supply Chain

1. **Enhanced Brand Reputation:** Consumers today are more informed and discerning. They often choose brands that align with their values. A supply chain grounded in Stoic ethics elevates the brand's reputation, making it more appealing to conscious consumers.

2. **Stakeholder Trust:** Stakeholders, including investors, employees, and partners, are more likely to trust and engage with businesses that operate ethically. By incorporating Stoic values into supply chain management, businesses can foster stronger, more trustful relationships with all its stakeholders.

3. **Long-term Success:** While unethical practices might offer short-term gains, they are not sustainable in the long run. On the other hand, a Stoic-aligned supply chain, focused on ethical considerations, ensures that the business remains resilient and successful over time.

Integrating Stoic ethics into supply chain management is not just a moral imperative; it's a strategic one. As businesses navigate the complexities of global operations, Stoic principles provide a steady compass, ensuring that every decision made aligns with both ethical standards and business objectives.

Resource Management and Stoic Frugality

Effective resource management is a cornerstone of successful business operations. However, in our modern era, the drive for growth often results in excessive consumption, leading to wasteful practices. Stoicism, with its emphasis on frugality and purpose, offers businesses a refreshing perspective on managing resources.

Stoic Frugality – More than Just Saving

Seneca once remarked, *"It is not the man who has too little, but the man who craves more, that is poor."* This isn't a call for businesses to scale down operations or curtail ambitions. Instead, it's an encouragement to approach resource allocation with discernment and intentionality. Stoic frugality is not about deprivation; it's about ensuring every resource, whether it's time, money, or materials, is used with a clear, beneficial purpose.

Purposeful Allocation

Drawing inspiration from Marcus Aurelius's insight, *"Very little is needed to make a happy life; it is all within yourself, in your way of thinking,"* businesses should adopt a minimalist approach to resource management. This means eliminating superfluous activities or expenditures that don't align with the company's core objectives or values. It's about optimising resources to derive maximum value, ensuring that every allocation serves a strategic and beneficial purpose.

Strategies for Waste Reduction

1. **Stoic Audits:** Regularly review and assess business processes to identify areas of waste or inefficiency. This reflects the Stoic practice of daily self-reflection, ensuring that operations remain lean and purposeful.

2. **Employee Training:** Incorporate Stoic principles into training programs, empowering employees to take ownership of resource management in their respective roles. By instilling Stoic values in employees, businesses can foster a culture where everyone is committed to judicious resource use.

3. **Sustainable Resource Utilisation:** Embrace sustainable practices, such as recycling or using renewable energy sources. This aligns with the Stoic emphasis on living in harmony with nature and ensures that the business treads lightly on the planet.

The Stoic Advantage

Businesses that incorporate Stoic frugality into their resource management strategies stand to gain a competitive edge. Not only do they enjoy cost savings from reduced waste, but they also cultivate a reputation for sustainability and ethical operations, which is increasingly valued in today's market.

In essence, Stoic principles challenge businesses to rethink resource management, moving away from unchecked consumption towards mindful, purposeful allocation. By doing so, businesses can ensure not only their own prosperity but also contribute positively to the wider world.

Feedback and Continuous Improvement: A Stoic Cycle

Feedback and continuous improvement are pivotal for any thriving business. Stoicism, with its emphasis on self-improvement, reflection, and embracing change as a natural part of existence, provides a unique lens through which businesses can cultivate an environment of growth and evolution.

The Stoic Embrace of Feedback

For Stoics, feedback isn't just about pointing out what's wrong but an opportunity for growth. As Marcus Aurelius aptly put it, *"If someone is able to show me that what I think or do is not right, I will happily change, for I seek the truth, by which no one was ever truly harmed."* In a business context, this translates to an open, non-defensive approach to feedback, viewing it as a tool for enhancement rather than criticism.

Operational Self-reflection

Just as Stoics advocate for daily reflection on one's actions and thoughts, businesses can adopt a similar practice at an operational level. Seneca's assertion, *"We should every night call ourselves to an account,"* can be mirrored in business through regular operational reviews. By periodically examining processes, strategies, and outcomes, companies can identify areas of improvement and make informed changes.

Techniques for Iterative Improvement

1. **Stoic Feedback Sessions:** Establish routine feedback sessions where teams can openly discuss operational challenges and successes. These sessions should be framed in a Stoic context, emphasising learning and growth over blame.

2. **Embrace Change as Natural:** Drawing from Epictetus's wisdom, *"Demand not that events should happen as you wish; but wish them to happen as they do happen, and you will go on well,"* businesses should view changes in operations, whether planned or unexpected, as natural and adjust strategies accordingly.

3. **Stoic Retrospectives:** At the end of significant projects or quarterly operations, conduct retrospectives. These are opportunities for teams to reflect on what went well, what

challenges arose, and how they can improve in the future, all through a Stoic lens.

4. **Data-driven Stoic Reflection:** Use data analytics to gauge operational effectiveness. By measuring and analysing outcomes, businesses can gain objective insights into their operations, allowing them to make Stoic-informed decisions on areas of improvement.

The Continuous Stoic Cycle
By fostering a Stoic-inspired feedback loop, businesses ensure that they're not just operating but continuously improving. This cycle of action, reflection, feedback, and adaptation creates an operational model that's both resilient and dynamic.

Adopting a Stoic approach to feedback and continuous improvement ensures that businesses remain agile, responsive, and always on a path of growth. It encourages a culture where feedback is not feared but embraced, and where every challenge is viewed as an opportunity for betterment.

Case Studies (Fictional):
Businesses Excelling in Stoic Operational Practices

The application of Stoic principles in business operations isn't just theoretical; numerous organisations have successfully integrated these ancient values into their daily practices, resulting in enhanced performance, employee satisfaction, and stakeholder trust. This section provides case studies that showcase the transformative power of Stoicism in business operations.

Case Study 1: Embracing Change in the Tech Industry

Background
TechSigma, a leading software development company, has been at the forefront of technological innovations for the past decade. With a diverse portfolio ranging from AI solutions to cloud computing, the company has always prided itself on its adaptability and responsiveness to market changes. But with rapid advancements come inevitable challenges, and the tech landscape's constant evolution means that companies must be prepared for unforeseen obstacles.

The Challenge
In 2022, TechSigma was gearing up for the launch of its most ambitious project yet: a cross-platform application designed to integrate various digital tools for businesses. The stakes were high, with significant investments in marketing and partnerships lined up for the launch. However, just weeks before the launch date, the development team identified a critical bug that compromised the application's security features.

The Stoic Response
Drawing inspiration from Epictetus's teaching, *"We cannot choose our external circumstances, but we can always choose how we respond to them,"* TechSigma's leadership reframed the challenge. Instead of viewing it as a disastrous setback, they saw it as an opportunity to demonstrate the company's commitment to quality and integrity.

1. **Transparent Communication:** The company immediately informed its stakeholders, including partners and early subscribers, about the delay. They provided a clear explanation of the issue, the steps they were taking to address it, and a revised timeline for the launch.

2. **Collaborative Problem Solving:** The development team, instead of working in silos, collaborated with external security experts to quickly address the bug. By pooling their expertise, they not only resolved the immediate issue but also enhanced the application's overall security framework.

3. **Employee Well-being:** Recognising the pressure on the development team, the company leadership provided additional resources and support, ensuring that employees didn't face burnout. Mental health professionals were brought in for counselling sessions, and the team was given time off once the issue was resolved.

Outcome

TechSigma's Stoic approach to the crisis was met with widespread appreciation. The transparent communication built deeper trust with their stakeholders. When the application was finally launched, it was met with positive reviews, particularly highlighting its robust security features. The incident, instead of being a blemish on the company's record, became a testament to its resilience, adaptability, and unwavering commitment to quality.

Reflection

TechSigma's experience underscores the transformative power of Stoicism in business operations. By maintaining a balanced perspective and focusing on proactive solutions, companies can turn potential setbacks into opportunities for growth and reinforcement of brand values.

Case Study 2: Sustainable Practices in the Fashion Industry

Background
EcoVogue, an up-and-coming fashion brand, has been making waves in the industry with its sustainable and eco-friendly clothing lines. With a mission to redefine fashion with environmental consciousness at its core, EcoVogue focuses on ethically sourced materials, minimal waste, and transparent manufacturing processes.

The Challenge
Despite its sustainable ethos, as EcoVogue grew in popularity, the demand for its products started to strain its supply chain. The brand faced a dilemma: how to scale production to meet increasing demand while still adhering to their foundational Stoic and sustainable values.

The Stoic Response:
Guided by Epictetus's wisdom, *"Don't explain your philosophy. Embody it,"* EcoVogue decided to double down on its commitment to sustainable practices, even if it meant slower growth.

1. **Ethical Sourcing:** Instead of shifting to more readily available but non-sustainable materials to meet demand, EcoVogue deepened partnerships with organic cotton farmers and eco-friendly dye suppliers. They also collaborated with artisan communities, ensuring fair wages and preserving traditional crafting techniques.

2. **Circular Fashion Model:** Embracing the Stoic principle of frugality and purpose, EcoVogue introduced a clothing recycling program. Customers could return used items from the brand in exchange for discounts on future purchases. These returned items were either refurbished and resold or recycled into new products.

3. **Consumer Education:** Recognising the role consumers play in sustainable fashion, EcoVogue launched campaigns to educate them about the environmental impact of their choices. Workshops, pop-up events, and digital content focused on slow fashion, the importance of quality over quantity, and the value of investing in timeless pieces.

Outcome
Though EcoVogue's decision to prioritise sustainability over rapid scalability initially led to slower delivery times and higher prices, their commitment resonated deeply with a growing segment of eco-conscious consumers. The brand's reputation for authenticity and quality bolstered its growth in the long run. Their circular fashion model not only reduced waste but also fostered brand loyalty, with customers valuing the brand's dedication to both the environment and the well-being of its suppliers.

Reflection
EcoVogue's journey is a testament to the enduring power of Stoic principles in guiding business decisions. In an industry often criticised for its environmental impact and fleeting trends, EcoVogue stands as a beacon, illustrating that businesses can thrive by staying true to their values and prioritising long-term impact over short-term gains.

Case Study 3: Building Resilient Leadership in Financial Services

Background
In the volatile realm of financial services, where economic fluctuations are the norm, a leading international bank, Alpha Finance, found itself on the brink of crisis following a major economic downturn. The sudden shift in the market left many

institutions scrambling, with some even facing bankruptcy. But for Alpha Finance, the challenge was met with a distinctly Stoic approach, and the results were nothing short of transformative.

The Challenge

Alpha Finance had always been a stalwart in the industry, but the rapid economic changes threatened its reputation and stability. Investors were wary, clients were pulling out, and there was palpable panic among the employees. The pressure on the leadership team was immense, not only to safeguard the company's assets but also to reassure its vast workforce and maintain stakeholder confidence.

The Stoic Response

Drawing from the wisdom of Seneca, who once said, *"Difficulties strengthen the mind, as labour does the body,"* the leadership at Alpha Finance saw the crisis not as a detrimental setback but as an opportunity to demonstrate resilience and fortify their operations.

1. **Transparent Communication:** Instead of keeping employees in the dark, the bank initiated open town-hall meetings, where leaders shared the current state of affairs and the strategic decisions being made. This transparency helped in alleviating anxiety and encouraged a collective spirit to face the challenges ahead.

2. **Client-Centric Approach:** Recognising the concerns of their clients, Alpha Finance set up dedicated communication lines, ensuring that clients had real-time updates and could make informed decisions about their investments.

3. **Operational Resilience:** The bank took rapid measures to streamline its operations, reduce non-essential expenses, and bolster its risk management strategies. This was not

just a reaction to the current crisis but a forward-looking approach to better handle future uncertainties.

4. **Employee Welfare:** Knowing that a motivated workforce was key to navigating the crisis, Alpha Finance introduced wellness programs and provided resources for mental health, recognising the strains such high-pressure situations could bring.

The Outcome
Alpha Finance emerged from the crisis stronger than before. Not only did they retain a significant portion of their clientele, but their transparent and ethical approach also attracted new clients who admired the bank's integrity during challenging times. Employees, too, felt a renewed sense of loyalty, appreciating the bank's commitment to its values and its people.

Reflection
In an industry often criticised for its short-term focus and reactive strategies, Alpha Finance's Stoic approach to leadership and crisis management showcased how ancient wisdom can offer timeless solutions. By viewing challenges as opportunities for growth and emphasising resilience, transparency, and ethics, the bank solidified its position as a true leader in the financial world.

Case Study 4: Enhancing Team Dynamics in Healthcare

Background
The healthcare sector is one of the most demanding industries, where the stakes are high, and the margin for error is minimal. At MedHeal Hospital, a renowned healthcare institution, the challenges were not just limited to patient care but also revolved around team dynamics. With a diverse

group of professionals working together under intense pressure, conflicts were inevitable. However, the Stoic philosophy provided a unique framework that transformed team interactions and enhanced patient outcomes.

The Challenge

MedHeal Hospital was facing issues of frequent disagreements among its multidisciplinary teams. Surgeons, nurses, technicians, and administrative staff often had different viewpoints, leading to delays in decision-making and, in some instances, compromised patient care. Morale was declining, and the attrition rate was on the rise.

The Stoic Response

The hospital's leadership decided to address the root cause of these conflicts, focusing on perception and response.

1. **Stoic Training Workshops:** MedHeal introduced a series of workshops where teams were introduced to Stoic principles. They were taught to differentiate between things they could control (their reactions, judgments) and things they couldn't (others' opinions, inherent challenges in patient cases).

2. **Interdisciplinary Collaboration:** Recognising that understanding and respect were crucial, the hospital organised interdisciplinary shadowing programs. For instance, administrators spent a day with surgeons, and technicians collaborated closely with nurses. This fostered empathy and a deeper understanding of each role's challenges and contributions.

3. **Reflective Practice:** Teams were encouraged to hold regular reflective sessions, where they discussed cases, not just from a medical perspective but also from a Stoic standpoint, evaluating their responses and judgments.

4. **Conflict Resolution Protocols:** Drawing from Stoicism, the hospital implemented a conflict resolution protocol that emphasised listening, understanding the underlying causes of disagreements, and finding common ground based on the shared goal of patient well-being.

The Outcome

The Stoic principles not only reduced conflicts but also fostered a collaborative and understanding environment at MedHeal. Teams started functioning more cohesively, and the patient care metrics, including recovery rates and patient satisfaction scores, saw a significant improvement. The attrition rate dropped, and MedHeal began to be recognised not just for its medical excellence but also for its harmonious and collaborative work environment.

Reflection

In an industry where team dynamics directly impact human lives, MedHeal's application of Stoicism serves as a testament to the philosophy's relevance and efficacy. By focusing on understanding, reflection, and control over one's reactions, the hospital was able to create a cohesive team that prioritised patient care above all else.

Synthesis and Learning

These case studies provide tangible examples of how Stoic principles can be seamlessly integrated into various business operations, yielding positive outcomes for both the organisations and their stakeholders. They serve as a testament to the universality and timeless relevance of Stoic wisdom, proving that these ancient teachings can indeed drive modern business success.

Conclusion: The Transformative Potential of Stoic-Driven Operations

The journey of integrating Stoic principles into daily business operations, as elaborated in this chapter, reveals a profound truth: businesses, irrespective of their size, industry, or model, stand to gain immeasurably from the wisdom of Stoicism. It's not just about making operations smoother or more efficient; it's about infusing every facet of business with purpose, resilience, and ethical grounding.

Seneca once remarked, *"It's not that we have a short time to live, but that we waste much of it."* This is particularly resonant in the business world. Time, resources, and human potential are often wasted in the pursuit of short-term goals or due to lack of clear direction. However, when operations are guided by Stoic principles, businesses can ensure that every action taken is purposeful and aligned with long-term objectives.

Another profound teaching comes from Epictetus, who said, *"Only the educated are free."* In the context of business, this emphasises the importance of continuous learning and adaptation. Just as Stoics believe in the constant evolution of self, businesses must continually evolve their operational strategies, always keeping Stoic teachings at their core. This ensures not only adaptability in the face of change but also a steadfast commitment to ethical and purpose-driven operations.

Finally, as Marcus Aurelius wisely observed, *"What we do now echoes in eternity."* The decisions businesses make, the strategies they employ, and the manner in which they operate have long-lasting impacts. By integrating Stoicism, businesses can ensure that their operational legacy is one of integrity, resilience, and positive impact.

In conclusion, the transformative potential of Stoic-driven operations is boundless. It offers a framework that goes beyond mere operational efficiency, touching upon the very ethos of what it means to conduct business. It is a call to action for businesses worldwide: to not only adopt Stoic principles in their day-to-day operations but to continually evolve with Stoicism at their heart, ensuring a legacy that is both impactful and enduring.

Chapter 10
Flourishing with Stoicism: A Recap and Future Outlook

As we stand on the cusp of concluding our exploration into the integration of Stoic principles in business, it's crucial to take a moment and glance back at the path we've traversed. Our journey began with an introduction to the core tenets of Stoicism, a philosophical doctrine birthed in the heart of ancient Greece and Rome. We delved into its foundational teachings, uncovering the wisdom of stoic sages like Epictetus, Seneca, and Marcus Aurelius. Their insights, though separated by millennia from our present time, resonated with the challenges and triumphs of the modern business landscape.

Understanding Stoicism in the realm of business was no mere theoretical exercise. It was a call to action, a beckoning to infuse our operational strategies, leadership styles, team dynamics, and more with the age-old wisdom of Stoicism. And as we journeyed through each chapter, we discovered that Stoicism is not a rigid framework but a malleable guide, adaptable to diverse business models and industries, from the tech giants of Silicon Valley to the local artisanal boutiques.

Now, as we prepare to explore this final chapter, we are poised to reflect on the transformative potential of Stoic-driven operations. The teachings we've explored are not just historical relics; they are living, breathing guidelines that can shape businesses, leaders, and teams for the better. Our aim is not only to summarise our learnings but to project into the future, envisioning a world where businesses, large and small, operate with Stoic teachings at their very core.

This chapter serves as both a culmination of our learnings and a beacon for what lies ahead. The world of business is ever-evolving, and as we stand on this precipice of reflection and anticipation, we are reminded of the enduring words of Seneca: *"As is a tale, so is life: not how long it is, but how good it is, is what matters."* Let's ensure the story of our businesses is not just about longevity but about the goodness and virtue we instil in every operational decision, guided by Stoicism's timeless principles.

Recap: Stoicism in Business 101

Stoic Foundations for Peak Performance
Stoicism, with its profound insights into human nature and the universe, offers a robust foundation for leadership and business operations. Seneca's wisdom resonates deeply here: *"It is quality rather than quantity that matters."* Instead of an endless pursuit of more, Stoicism teaches businesses to focus on delivering quality in all endeavours, be it in products, services, or relationships.

Achieving Virtuous Leadership and Decision-making
Epictetus once remarked, *"Men are disturbed not by things, but by the view which they take of them."* This emphasises the essence of perspective in leadership. Business leaders, guided by Stoic principles, learn to view challenges as opportunities, ensuring decisions are not just commercially viable but also ethically sound.

Resilience at the Business Summit
Resilience remains a key cornerstone in Stoicism. Drawing from Seneca's observation, *"Difficulties strengthen the mind, as labour does the body,"* we delved into how businesses can harness adversities to forge stronger operational frameworks and resilient mindsets. In business, this translates to

navigating market challenges with unwavering determination, always ready to innovate and adapt.

The Pursuit of Simplicity for Efficient Outcomes
Simplicity and focus are paramount in Stoic teachings. As Epictetus puts it, *"Make the best use of what is in your power, and take the rest as it happens."* This principle encourages businesses to declutter, streamline operations, and focus on what truly matters, ensuring resources are optimally utilised.

Empathetic Leadership and Team Cohesion
The importance of understanding and compassion shines brightly in Stoicism. Drawing from Marcus Aurelius's counsel, *"Whenever you are about to find fault with someone, ask yourself the following question: What fault of mine most nearly resembles the one I am about to criticise?"* it reminds leaders of the power of empathy. Integrating this into business operations fosters team cohesion, reduces conflict, and builds trust.

The Crucial Role of Stoicism in Modern Business Practices
Stoic philosophy's enduring wisdom has proven its relevance repeatedly in the modern business landscape. In a world where business dynamics shift rapidly, Stoic principles guide organisations to act with integrity, purpose, and a long-term vision. As Seneca aptly stated, *"A good character, when it is once settled and perfected, will shine through."* Similarly, businesses that embed Stoic values into their ethos not only thrive commercially but also stand out as beacons of ethical and sustainable practices.

The Stoic Legacy in Today's Business Landscape

Stoic Transformations in Business

The Stoic philosophy, with its emphasis on virtue, wisdom, courage, and moderation, has been a guiding light for businesses aiming for peak performance and leadership. In the tumultuous world of modern commerce, where market dynamics are ever-evolving and uncertainties abound, Stoic principles act as a compass. They steer businesses towards ethical decisions, resilient strategies, and a focus on genuine value creation rather than fleeting gains.

Companies that have internalised Stoic teachings often find themselves more adaptable in the face of change. They prioritise long-term sustainability over short-term profits and place a high value on the well-being of their employees and stakeholders. This not only earns them respect in the industry but also engenders trust among consumers and partners. As the Stoic philosopher Seneca advised, *"It is not the man who has too little, but the man who craves more, that is poor."* Businesses that heed this counsel find richness not in mere profits but in the depth of their relationships, the quality of their products, and the impact they make in the world.

Successes Born from Stoicism

Many success stories in the business landscape can be attributed to the silent influence of Stoic principles. One such example is a tech startup that, despite facing severe competition and dwindling resources, persisted in its mission by focusing on what was within its control and accepting external factors with equanimity. Drawing inspiration from Epictetus's wisdom, *"We cannot choose our external circumstances, but we can always choose how we respond to them,"* the startup pivoted its strategy, fostered a culture of continuous learning, and eventually emerged as an industry leader.

Another tale of Stoic influence is evident in a global manufacturing company that faced a major ethical dilemma. Instead of opting for a cost-effective but environmentally harmful process, the company, inspired by Marcus Aurelius's assertion, *"Do what is necessary, and whatever the reason of a social animal naturally requires, and as it requires,"* chose a more sustainable approach. This not only preserved the environment but also positioned the company as a frontrunner in sustainable practices, earning it accolades and consumer trust.

In the finance sector, a leading investment firm, grounded in Stoic values, always prioritised its clients' long-term benefits over immediate returns. This philosophy, mirroring Seneca's insight, *"True happiness is to enjoy the present, without anxious dependence upon the future,"* led the firm to make prudent investment choices, ensuring steady growth and securing its position as a trusted advisor.

These narratives underscore the power and relevance of Stoicism in today's business world. They serve as testimonials to the transformative potential of ancient wisdom in contemporary settings, proving that the path to the summit, even in business, is paved with Stoic principles.

Challenges and Triumphs

Navigating the Rough Terrains with Stoicism
Incorporating Stoic principles into the business arena is not without its challenges. The corporate world, driven by fast-paced innovations, competitive pressures, and an ever-changing consumer landscape, often clashes with Stoic ideals of patience, reflection, and long-term vision. Executives might grapple with the dichotomy of pushing for rapid growth while staying true to the Stoic emphasis on moderation and

purposeful action. As the Stoic philosopher Epictetus stated, *"Difficulties are things that show a person what they are."* In the realm of business, these difficulties test the mettle of organisations and their commitment to Stoic values.

For instance, in the sales-driven sectors, the relentless pursuit of quarterly targets may sometimes overshadow the Stoic counsel of ethical dealings and building genuine relationships. Similarly, in the highly competitive tech industry, the race to be the first-to-market might challenge the Stoic principle of accepting outcomes beyond one's control.

Triumphing Over Adversities with Stoic Resilience

Yet, for businesses that remain unwavering in their Stoic commitments, the challenges are not endpoints but mere bends in their journey to the summit. By embodying the Stoic teachings, companies discover an unmatched reservoir of resilience and adaptability. The very challenges that seem insurmountable become opportunities for growth and reflection.

Consider the example of a global retail brand that, amidst a market downturn, chose to view the scenario not as a setback but as a Stoic test of its values and adaptability. Drawing from Seneca's wisdom, *"Fire tests gold, suffering tests brave men,"* the brand revamped its strategies, focusing on ethical sourcing, community engagement, and long-term sustainability. This Stoic-inspired pivot not only helped the brand weather the downturn but also established it as an industry benchmark for ethical and sustainable practices.

Similarly, a multinational corporation, faced with a public relations crisis, leaned into the Stoic principle of taking responsibility for one's actions. Instead of deflecting blame, the corporation, inspired by Marcus Aurelius's reminder, *"The best revenge is not to be like your enemy,"* acknowledged its mistakes, made amends, and took proactive steps to prevent future mishaps. This transparent and responsible approach not only salvaged the company's reputation but also strengthened its bond with stakeholders.

Celebrating the Stoic Milestones
The journey of integrating Stoicism into business operations is filled with both challenges and moments of triumph. These milestones, whether they are overcoming a market slump, forging a new ethical path, or simply making decisions grounded in Stoic wisdom, are worth celebrating. They serve as reminders of the transformative power of Stoicism and the peaks that businesses can achieve when ancient principles guide their modern endeavours.

In the grand tapestry of business leadership and peak performance, Stoicism shines as a golden thread, weaving together tales of challenges faced, lessons learned, and summits conquered. The journey might be arduous, but for those with Stoic principles at their core, the view from the summit is unparalleled.

The Road Ahead: Stoicism in a Rapidly Evolving World

Stoicism Amidst a Dynamic Business Landscape
The business world, much like life itself, is in a state of perpetual flux. With technological advances, shifting consumer behaviours, and global challenges, businesses are constantly at the intersection of transformation and adaptation. Yet, as the environment evolves, the core tenets of Stoicism remain as relevant as ever. The Stoic teachings, deeply rooted in understanding one's own nature and the nature of the universe, provide a timeless compass for navigating this dynamic landscape. As Seneca wisely observed, *"While we are postponing, life speeds by."* In the context of business, this serves as a reminder for companies

to be proactive, adaptive, and anchored in their core values amidst change.

Stoicism in the Age of Artificial Intelligence

One of the most transformative forces in the modern business world is Artificial Intelligence (AI). As AI-driven solutions become integral to decision-making, there's a burgeoning need for ethical considerations. Stoicism, with its emphasis on virtue, moral integrity, and the betterment of society, can offer invaluable guidance in this domain. Implementing AI without compromising on ethical values requires a Stoic balance of technological prowess with moral responsibility. As companies venture further into the AI frontier, Stoic principles can help ensure that these advancements benefit humanity at large, rather than causing unintended harm.

Sustainability: The Stoic's Long Game

Another critical frontier for businesses is sustainability. In an age where short-term gains often overshadow long-term impacts, the Stoic emphasis on thinking for the collective good and future generations becomes paramount. Drawing from the Stoic principle of living in harmony with nature, businesses can champion sustainable practices that not only ensure their longevity but also protect the planet. As Epictetus remarked, *"We are not given complete control,"* reminding businesses of the finite resources at their disposal and the responsibility to use them judiciously.

Remote Work Dynamics and Stoic Harmony

The recent global events have catalysed a shift towards remote work, challenging traditional business operations and team dynamics. As companies grapple with this new norm, Stoicism offers insights into maintaining harmony, cohesion, and productivity. Marcus Aurelius's assertion, *"People exist for one another,"* underscores the importance of fostering connections, even in virtual spaces. With the shift to remote work, it's crucial for leaders to ensure that teams feel valued, connected, and integrated into the company's larger mission.

Employing Stoic wisdom, businesses can create environments where employees, irrespective of their physical location, feel a deep sense of belonging and purpose.

The Stoic Beacon for the Future

As businesses venture into the uncharted terrains of the future, the teachings of Stoicism stand as a beacon, guiding them towards ethical decisions, sustainable operations, and harmonious team dynamics. Whether it's the ethical dilemmas posed by AI, the environmental responsibilities underlined by sustainability, or the challenges of remote work, Stoic principles provide a robust framework for businesses to thrive.

As the world continues its rapid pace of change, the age-old wisdom of Stoicism remains a steadfast guide. Businesses that choose to embody these ancient principles are not only poised for peak performance but also for meaningful, purpose-driven leadership. With Stoicism at the helm, businesses can ensure that their journey, no matter how tumultuous, is always towards the summit of ethical and sustainable success.

The Next Steps for Business Leaders

Crafting a Stoic Leadership Blueprint

To truly embody Stoicism at the summit of business leadership, it's vital to craft a strategic blueprint that intertwines Stoic principles with daily operations. This doesn't merely mean referencing Stoic quotes in board meetings but involves a deep-rooted integration of Stoicism in decision-making, team dynamics, and long-term visions. As Marcus Aurelius once said, *"The best revenge is to be unlike him who performed the injury."* In the cutthroat world of business, this Stoic sentiment encourages leaders to rise above petty rivalries and instead focus on ethical and sustainable growth.

Building a Stoic Learning Culture

Continuous learning lies at the heart of Stoicism. Business leaders can foster a culture where employees are encouraged to delve into Stoic teachings regularly. This could involve setting up monthly Stoic book clubs, inviting philosophers for guest lectures, or even creating online Stoic learning modules tailored for the business context. By instilling a culture of Stoic learning, businesses can ensure that their teams are equipped with the philosophical tools to navigate both professional and personal challenges.

Stoic Reflection and Adaptation

One of the core tenets of Stoicism is the importance of self-reflection. Business leaders can integrate this by setting aside dedicated time for Stoic reflection, both at an individual and organisational level. This could mean quarterly retreats focused on Stoic teachings or even weekly reflection sessions where teams discuss their challenges and learnings in the light of Stoic wisdom. Such practices ensure that the business remains adaptive and aligned with Stoic principles, even as it grows and evolves.

Engaging with the Stoic Community

The global Stoic community is vibrant and ever-evolving. Business leaders can benefit immensely by engaging with this community, attending Stoic conferences, participating in forums, and even collaborating on Stoic business projects. Such engagements offer fresh perspectives and provide a platform for leaders to share their own experiences of integrating Stoicism into their businesses.

Measurement and Evolution

As with any strategic initiative, the integration of Stoicism into business operations must be measurable. Leaders can establish Stoic KPIs (Key Performance Indicators) to track the impact of Stoic practices on team morale, decision-making, and overall business performance. Regularly measuring against these KPIs ensures that the business remains on the right Stoic path and can adapt its strategies as needed.

The journey of integrating Stoicism into business operations is continuous and ever-evolving. By grounding their ambitions in Stoic contentment and virtue, business leaders can truly achieve peak performance and leadership, driving their organisations to new summits of success.

The Wider Impact: Beyond Business

Stoic Businesses as Pillars of Society
The Stoic philosophy emphasises virtue and wisdom as the highest goods. When businesses, which are integral components of society, integrate these Stoic principles, they can transition from being mere economic entities to pillars that uphold and advance societal values. Epictetus reminded us that *"Wealth consists not in having great possessions, but in having few wants."* A business rooted in Stoicism would, therefore, prioritise societal well-being over unchecked growth, ensuring its actions align with the broader good.

Community Growth through Stoic Values
Companies that operate under Stoic principles can significantly influence their communities. By promoting virtues such as wisdom, courage, and justice in their operations, they set a benchmark for ethical practices. Local businesses might be inspired to adopt similar values, leading to an ecosystem where companies prioritise the well-being of the community. This could manifest in various ways - from providing fair wages and ensuring employee well-being to supporting local initiatives and promoting community engagement.

Sustainability and Stoicism
The Stoic teaching of living in accordance with nature resonates deeply with the modern need for sustainable

business practices. Businesses that internalise this teaching understand the importance of harmonising their operations with the environment. This means adopting eco-friendly practices, reducing waste, and investing in sustainable technologies. By doing so, they not only ensure their longevity but also contribute to the preservation of our planet. Businesses have the opportunity to leave a lasting, positive imprint on the earth.

Championing Social Responsibility
Stoic businesses recognise their role in the larger societal framework and understand the interconnectedness of all actions. By emphasising social responsibility, they can address societal challenges proactively, be it through philanthropic efforts, educational initiatives, or supporting marginalised communities. Such businesses become beacons of hope and exemplify the Stoic belief in the brotherhood of humanity.

Inspiring a New Wave of Ethical Entrepreneurs
The ripple effect of Stoic-driven businesses is profound. As they lead by example, they inspire a new generation of entrepreneurs to build ventures rooted in Stoic principles. This new wave of businesses, with a foundation in ancient wisdom, can redefine the future landscape, emphasising ethical growth, community well-being, and global harmony. In essence, while the primary aim of **"Stoicism at the Summit"** is to guide businesses towards peak performance and leadership, the broader vision is a world where businesses, rooted in Stoic principles, act as catalysts for positive societal transformation. The true summit, as envisioned by Stoic philosophy, is a world where businesses thrive, not at the expense of society, but in harmony with it.

Concluding Thoughts: A Call to Stoic Action

Revisiting the Pinnacle of Stoic Business

As we stand at the summit, looking back at the journey undertaken, it's evident how Stoic principles have been the bedrock of sustainable success in business. Businesses that dare to integrate Stoicism not only navigate challenges with fortitude but also set themselves apart in an ever-competitive landscape.

The Timeless Tenets of Stoicism in Business

From the teachings of Marcus Aurelius to the insights of Epictetus, the Stoic philosophy offers timeless wisdom. In an age defined by rapid technological advancements and unpredictable market shifts, Stoicism provides the anchor. It reminds businesses to focus on what they can control, to act justly, and to approach challenges with a balanced mind. This age-old wisdom is not just a philosophical discourse but a practical guide for modern businesses aiming for peak performance.

Championing the Stoic Legacy

Every business has the potential to leave a legacy. Stoic businesses, however, ensure that this legacy is one of purpose, resilience, and ethical excellence. By championing Stoicism, businesses can redefine success – not as mere profit generation, but as meaningful impact. They can inspire stakeholders, from employees to customers, to adopt a Stoic way of life, creating ripples of positive change.

A Vision for the Future

Looking ahead, the call to Stoic action is not just for the present moment but for the future of business. In a world where businesses play a pivotal role in shaping societies, the integration of Stoic principles ensures that this shaping is for the collective good. It's a vision where businesses rise above short-term gains, focusing on long-term value creation, ethical leadership, and societal well-being.

An Invitation to Embrace the Stoic Path
As **"Stoicism at the Summit"** draws to a close, the journey, in many ways, is just beginning. Business leaders and entrepreneurs are invited to embrace Stoicism, not as a temporary strategy but as a lifelong commitment. It's a commitment to lead with wisdom, act with integrity, and create a legacy that future generations will look upon with admiration and gratitude.

In the words of Marcus Aurelius, *"The best revenge is not to be like your enemy."* In the realm of business, this translates to not being swayed by fleeting trends but being grounded in the eternal wisdom of Stoicism. Let this be the beacon that guides businesses to the true summit – one of purpose, resilience, and unparalleled excellence.

About the Authors

Greig Calder
Greig Calder is a consultant business architect and business analyst. He is a Certified Business Architect (CBA)® with the Business Architecture Guild and has been a member of the Guild since 2015. He has a diploma in business analysis from the British Computer Society and has been providing business architecture and business analysis services to clients since 2006. He is also a certified project manager (PRINCE2 Practitioner), and has an honours degree in town planning from the University of Strathclyde Business School (1990). Previous clients include organisations in banking, investment management, utilities, human resources, and both central and local government departments and agencies.

Kirsten Calder
Kirsten Calder is an artist with over thirty years experience that includes working for corporate and private clients.

Printed in Great Britain
by Amazon

36049928R00106